Created by Jodi Dee.
Logo and image designs by Nicole Hargrove. Cover design by Magnetic, LLC.
Photography by Jodi Dee & Red Mailbox Media.
Create a Home of Learning and associated trademarks, images, photographs, and trade dress are
owned by Jodi Dee Publishing.
www.jodidee.com.

Published in USA, 2020
Printed in Canada by Friesens Corporation

Library of Congress Control Number: ISBN-13: 978-0-9985277-5-8

DEDICATION

To my mother, Cecile Tousignant,
who has dedicated her life to the education of young children.

PREFACE

The photographs included in this book were candid, and taken over the last thirteen years raising my three children (other than the still pictures of products).

Through the images you will see my children grow in front of you, that I used all the concepts and resources discussed in this book (for over a decade), and continue to use many to this day. At the time, I had no idea I would ever use these photos (except personally) - so please excuse some of the quality!

I also did not structure this book like a traditional book on purpose. There are no numbered Chapters or Indices, nor is it designed to be linear (just like learning)! Start by setting up one learning area or three. Do what resonates with you and your child(ren). Follow their rhythm!

Each learning area has a free online video with additional images and video clips at jodiee.com < Parenting/Children < Create a Home of Learning or YOUTUBE < Jodi Dee.

I hope you enjoy creating your own home of learning!

Contents

Preface...4

Introduction..7

PART I...11

The Program...12

Children Learn While They Play...15

Types of Play..16

How a Child Plays...17

Preschool Versus Creating a Home of Learning................................19

Stay at Home Parents Versus Working Parents.................................21

Influencing Factors, Interests, & Differing Abilities........................22

Areas of Learning & Learning Connections 27

Language...30

Cognitive...33

Physical...38

Social & Emotional 43

PART I-II...48

The Playroom 49

Types of Toys & Equipment...56

Open-Ended Toys...57

Structured Toys..61

Creating Collections...63

Playroom Guidelines...65

Preparedness...69

Transition Time..70

Role of Facilitator...71

PART II..76

Play & Learning Areas in the Home..............................77

12 Learning Areas..79

Center Activity Table..81

House Area...90

Climbing & Movement Area...109

Playhouse Area...114

Art Area..117

Reading Area..125

Writing Area...132

Listening Area...137

Construction & Block Area...143

Dollhouse Area..149

Sensory Table...154

Outdoor Area..162

PART III...168

QUICK GUIDE: Rotation of Toys & Learning Areas.............169

How to Structure a Day Suggestions..............................170

A Typical Day...171

Homemade Playdough Recipe.......................................173

Suggestions to Purchase Toys & Equipment.....................174

Resources..175

GLOSSARY...176

References...180

Acknowledgement..182

About the Author...183

More Books by Author Jodi Dee....................................184

Introduction

A child's brain triples in size during the first three years of life and absorbs more information during that period than any other time, <u>and</u> ninety percent of a child's brain is developed by age five. It is during

this time that a child is prepared for all future experiences, interpretations, and critical thinking in their upcoming lives. This early stage in a child's life establishes the basis for confidence, understanding, and independence, as well as a joy for learning.

As parents, we can incorporate this knowledge into our everyday routines, to enhance and fulfill the needs of our developing child(ren), starting at birth. We can set up a learning environment right in our homes, that provides rich discovery and exploration, and lays the necessary foundation of all future learning. **Children learn while they play.**

I didn't realize I had this answer until I started scheduling play dates with other moms who constantly asked questions about what I was doing, why, and how. People often commented that my three children were independent, competent, and capable. They would marvel at my children's play-

room and the toys I had for them. Their children would enter eagerly and get right to play.

I could easily have six children in my playroom at one time, all busy and having fun without conflict, which usually turned into an elaborate game or play scenario, like pretending to run a restaurant. After one visit with another mother of three, who asked

if I would show her how to set up her home, I decided to start blogging on the topic. This led to writing articles for Bay State Parent magazine, and finally this book.

I grew up in a perfect storm. It was loud and chaotic, but full of excitement and energy every day. I grew up in an early learning center that my mother started when I was two years old. I was a student, participant, observer, helper, facilitator, and eventually worked in the center. I did everything from creating activities, painting and cleaning in the summers, to filling baggies of treats on different holidays.

I grew up exposed to and part of every scenario you could imagine, ranging from observing behavioral problems, to developing techniques to improve them. I also worked with bilingual children who couldn't speak English to engaging children in fun activities using homemade play dough. My childhood was full of limitless, complex, and rich opportunities to explore and learn. If I wanted to "play", I could go outside to the 12,000 square foot playground or into the 2,000 square foot preschool, set up with

learning centers, attached to our home.

There were always other children playing and friends to socialize with. I was fortunate in my youth to have such freedom to explore and discover, in any play area at any time. My favorite areas were the doll house corner, slide-house climbing structure, indoor bike riding area, a massive stand-up indoor sandbox, and a real stage where I would set up elaborate cities of Fisher price houses and Playskool peoples. Before the age of seven I had been exposed to more opportunities for learning than most children ever have.

As a child, my world was "Busy Bees Preschool Center". My mother's life revolved around research, learning, and building a top-notch program. Her teaching style evolved based on the newest research, proven tech-

niques, and ways to maximize opportunities for learning. My mother sold her successful business after thirty five years. Her business had started as a part time center but became one of the leading schools in the area, and still is to this day. My mother now consults for the state and other private programs, including her old center.

I witnessed and absorbed all this growing up in a preschool. To this day, people of all ages who attended my mother's preschool stop her to recall memories about their time at "Busy Bees". I remember my years in preschool over any other grade, even college. I remember details as though it were yesterday. I remember being three years old and playing the farmer's

wife in a nursery rhyme performance of the Three Blind Mice. I remember walking up my street in a parade as a stuffed pumpkin. The preschool was my little world, a safe place to create my own reality with all the right toys.

From the age of two through my college years I absorbed every facet of early childhood and the details of running a center, from being the student in the curriculum, to running it. I experienced most techniques and practices without even realizing it, until

I became a parent myself. I incorporated this knowledge into my home and the every day lives of my children, and continue to do so in many ways (even though my children are now thirteen, eleven, and ten).

What I was exposed to I consciously replicated, to provide my children a similar experience that I had as a child. I used similar toys and spaces to explore, and encouraged them to be physically active and creative. I staged a home for them to learn and develop in!

Even children who eventually attend a full-day preschool spend more time at home than anywhere else, and by setting up the right types of play, you too can create your own home of learning!

PART I

THE PROGRAM

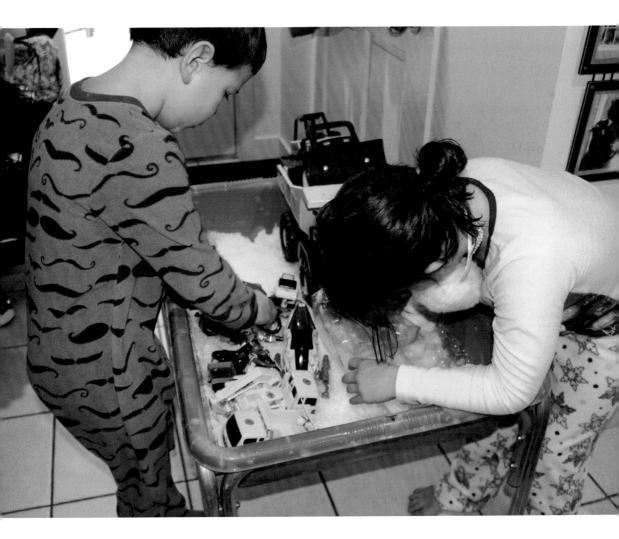

This program can be started as soon as a child can crawl, throughout a child's elementary school years. Understanding how children learn and play, the different types of toys and techniques to engage and facilitate play, will transform the lives of your children and open the world of learning and discovery right in your home.

You will see your child's excitement every time he or she enters the playroom and different learning areas. You will recognize how your child learns and develops. You will watch your child grow into a competent, confident, independent, and prepared learner while playing and having fun.

Many concepts, materials, and activities in this book have been developed and used by early childhood practitioners and educators for decades, and are implemented and in practice in nationally accredited early learning programs. Parents can offer the same rich experiences and create the same environment at home.

By following the simple instructions, using the lists of toys and equipment, diagrams, and pictures, you can easily create your own home of learning!

THIS PROGRAM PROVIDES:

- A simple, easy to follow format
- An organized and structured way to engage in your child's development
- The right toys, supplies, and equipment to promote learning
- Important milestones to consider as your child grows
- Guidelines to set up play and learning areas
- Meaningful, concrete, and screen-free activities
- Steps to facilitate proper growth and development
- School preparedness and competency

Children Learn While They Play

Child development experts agree that play is integral to learning and that children learn the most when caretakers and teachers are trained in understanding how play contributes to learning. Accredited early learning centers use resources and space to facilitate the right types of play.

What a child plays with and how matters during the different stages of his or her development. The right types of play builds the foundation of math, problem solving, literacy, social skills, art and creativity, science concepts, emotional maturity, critical thinking, leadership, and more.

Play is not a break from learning, it's the way children learn.

CHILDREN IN A HOME OF LEARNING WILL...

- **Grow to be independent**
- **Develop self-confidence**
- **Learn to play by themselves or with a friend**
- **Gain skills and abilities in daily activities**
- **Make choices on their own**
- **Learn to explore with intention**
- **Make the transition to school easier**
- **Gain understanding of the world around them**

Types of Play

There are three terms frequently used to describe play: free play, structured play, and unstructured play. All are important in learning and development. This book focuses on these types of play and how to use and set-up these types of play in a home setting.

STRUCTURED PLAY is an activity that has a set of rules and a set outcome, that is pre-determined.

A puzzle, matching game, or board game, are examples of structured play. Another is giving a child a craft with a set outcome, such as making a paper snowman. This art activity is guided by a parent or caregiver. A child is provided a paper cutout of the body of a snowman, with buttons for eyes, a hat, or other accessories (stick for a broom, small orange triangles for a nose, and so forth). A sample snowman is provided as a model. The child is encouraged to follow the sample with the materials provided, and can ask for help when it is needed.

FREE PLAY is time during the day where a child can play at their leisure and freely explore the toys, games, and activities set out and available to them, undirected (by an adult).

UNSTRUCTURED PLAY is when a child is provided toys or materials (usually manipulatives or open-ended toys), to use or do whatever they choose (in a safe way). For example, giving them moon sand to mold or building blocks to build with. This is also sometimes called "free play".

How a Child Plays

Play is both simple and complex. How a child plays depends on a child's age, interest, and developmental level.

The attention span of a child will vary by age. A younger child's attention span (between six months and three-years-old), can be very short (anywhere between five to fifteen minutes), and he or she will cycle through different play areas often. Older children (between four and seven), will play longer (twenty minutes to an hour), and the play will be more engaged and complex.

Many use the rule 'two to five minutes per age' (so a five-year-old could stay focussed on a task for ten to twenty five minutes).

However, there is a misconception that if a child only plays with something for five minutes, he or she is bored, it isn't challenging enough, or the child isn't interested in it. A child will often play with something five minutes, drop it, go do something else for ten minutes, then return to the prior activity again. This is the nature of free play! But, always use your judgment. If your child seems bored or has mastered an activity (especially a structured toy or activity), for example, a 20-piece puzzle, it may be time to upgrade the level of the toy to a 50-piece puzzle.

It is normal behavior for a child to play alone (**solitary or independent play**). Even if other children are in the same room many children just prefer to play by themselves. **How a child plays with other children will change as he or she grows.**

PARALLEL PLAY (between one and three) is when a child will stand near or alongside another child but not engage in play with that child. The child will simply stand nearby, play with his or her own toy, and observe what the other child is doing at the same time.

ASSOCIATE PLAY (between three and four) is when a child will stand next to another child, and sometimes interact (want the other child's car or make a comment), but will continue to play independently and observe what the other child is doing.

COOPERATIVE PLAY (four and older) is when children start to play together. Two boys may pretend to be monster trucks in a monster truck show, they may build towers and crash their cars into each other's towers, or work together to build a tower to knock down.

Preschool Versus Creating a Home of Learning

My children all attended partial day preschool programs, starting at the recommended age of two and a half. The programs were two days a week, four hours a day. They then progressed to three days a week, for ages four and older. There were five-day, full day programs available, but I felt attending a full day program was best started in kindergarten.

I strongly believe children should attend an accredited preschool program when possible, and in no way does creating a home of learning replace this experience. Accredited preschools follow a plan that balances child-choice activities with academic based teacher-led activities (for example, learning and writing a different letter of the alphabet each week, the months

of the year, and more).

Much of what is taught in this book is used and set up in accredited centers, but are part of an annual plan that is structured and designed against the Curriculum Frameworks of early childhood standards. Preschool is designed to prepare a child for instruction-based learning.

Children also need the social and emotional exposure for proper development that can be achieved by attending and interacting in group settings. Participating in a program with other children and adults is extremely important.

A parent can easily implement and follow a curriculum with this setup, but instruction generally works best for older children (five-years-old and up), when they are developmentally ready for school full time.

If a parent is homeschooling, he or she can easily apply more structured use of the learning areas described, and weave in more structure and adult-led activities.

Setting up different spaces establishes a natural environment of play and learning, and changing it regularly keeps it new and interesting. How a parent uses these learning areas, whether before school, after school, or as "school" is up to her or him!

Stay at Home Parents Versus Working Parents

This program works very well for working parents or stay at home parents. Once the learning areas are established and rotating the toys and equipment has become routine, the setup of this program should require less than fifteen minutes a day. The learning areas and toys can be used anytime the children are home.

A stay at home parent can use this system as part of a homeschool program, or simply to keep their young children occupied and learning throughout the day, until they attend preschool or school full time.

Full-time working parents can use this system for their children before and after day care, or used by a babysitter or nanny if they are cared for in the home.

A child who is home for ten hours a day will require much more stimuli, equipment, toys, and activities than one who is at preschool or day care for four to eight hours a day.

A grandparent, babysitter, or nanny can follow this routine when they arrive or before the children come home from school. This book can be given as a guide. He or she will find these resources helpful to keep the children happy and having fun. You will also have the peace of mind knowing your children are playing and learning.

Once a home is equipped with the right setup and toys, it simply comes down to an adult rotating material in and out, and to organize and encourage play.

I would set up my playroom every evening after the children went to sleep. I loved watching them wake up and run downstairs as though it were Christmas morning, eager to see the playroom with "new" toys to play with and explore. They ran to the playroom ready to "work". I am not sure why, but at some point, we started calling the play or activities "jobs", and to this day they find challenges and "working" (like schoolwork) fun. This also made the transition to formal schooling much easier. On days I was too tired or forgot to set up the play area, my middle daughter would often remind me or ask, "Mommy, what jobs can I do today?" Or, she would simply go get the bin of toys she wanted to play with on her own. This really becomes a system, and a way of life for young children at home.

When my children started school full time, I set up the playroom for before and after school, so when they came home, they had constructive and imaginative play waiting. It balanced the restrictions of being in a classroom, having to be quiet, and standing in lines, when there was the inherent need for freedom and movement! After sitting most of the day, being able to come home to a playroom full of opportunity provided the children with the independence to move their bodies at their own pace and do whatever they chose. It supplemented the academic with necessary creativity and fun.

The most important thing is to let the children play, set up the right environment, and provide them with the right resources to do so each day.

Influencing Factors Interests, and Differing Abilities

All children are alike, and all children are different. Some will naturally be drawn to and play with certain types of toys or equipment more than others. Some children may spend most of the day playing with manipulatives (like building blocks or cars). Other children will prefer the Reading Area of Learning and spend their time looking at books. **Refer to PART II: Reading Area.**

Learning is influenced by many factors; genetic heritage, age, size, gender, culture (both home and community), interests, and differeing abilities, and medical conditions. These factors are very important to consider in what you can expect from a child. Educators refer to these differences as "**developmental ranges**".

One child may utter words by twelve months and not yet be walking, while another may be walking at ten months but not speak their first words until eighteen months. This does not mean one child is smarter, more athletic, or more advanced than the other. It may just mean that one child is developing faster in the area of language, and the other in the area of physical development.

What a child can be expected to do will be influenced by age and size. For example, a three-year-old can stand on one foot but not hop on one foot. Some four-year olds can print some letters of the alphabet whereas a five-year-old can print a word - CAT.

Another example is a boy who is overweight will have more difficulty running than a boy of the same height and age who is not. Adults may expect higher motor skills from a three-year-old girl who looks older because she is taller and expect less motor skills from a four-year-old boy is shorter.

Gender also influences learning. Typically, girls develop faster than boys physically, including their brains and nervous systems. But boys tend to have more muscle and are generally lighter in bone mass and weight. This is why many boys are quicker and stronger in physical games and activities than girls in early years.

You will also notice that girls are generally more developed in fine motor skills than boys of the same age, and have more interest in those activities (such as coloring, writing, and tasks like puzzles).

But, be careful not to stereotype!

Boys and girls have consistent play styles and interests (Maccoby, 2002)

The belief that boys do not play with dolls or girls do not play with cars are examples of gender stereotypes. They each will play with both if the options are available! Girls and boys both need exposure to all learning areas and activities.

GENDER GUIDELINES TO CONSIDER:

GIRLS...

- **Prefer inside play**
- **Play in smaller groups** (two or three)
- **Are more cooperative**
- **Show affection to peers with touch** (holding hands, hugging, kissing)
- **More readily show caring and empathy**
- **In conflict, will "give the cold shoulder"**
- **Like to be close to adults**
- **Enjoy playing social themes** (family, school, dress, caring)

BOYS...

- **Prefer outdoor play**
- **Play in larger groups** (three or more)
- **Are more physical**
- **Show affection by punching or exhibiting rowdy behavior**
- **Are more competitive**
- **Act out by using physical strength**
- **Avoid being close to adult when at play**
- **Like action** (danger, heroism)

Most differing physical abilities will be self evident, and you can adjust your setup to accommodate. For example, wheelchair access will require more space to move, a higher worktable, and so on.

However, some differing abilities are not obvious. Often a child who has difficulty hearing or seeing goes unnoticed, because no demands have been placed on him or her yet in that area.

Another example is when a child has noticeable difficulty sticking to a task. It may not automatically be hyperactivity or ADD (attention deficit

disorder). Research has indicated that less than 10% of the population actually have this condition. In many cases, the inability to settle down or focus on a task may be the child hasn't been given enough time to adjust from the structure of school to home, between activities, or that child is simply not getting enough physical activity. **Refer to Part I-II: Transition Time.** Children have an immense amount of energy that they need to release every day!

Some children may need practice in coordination (such as swinging a bat or pumping a swing), while others may need practice with fine motor skills (holding and writing with a pencil). If a child needs work in one area you can guide him or her to that activity.

Offering various choices in activities will give you insight into your child's developmental progress, interests and abilities, and you can easily adjust and change the setup to accommodate them.

Areas of Learning & Learning Connections

Research on brain development has found that the brain develops at the fastest rate during the first three years of life, in size and connections, and continues through adolescence.

"Connections" refer to the way a brain takes in and processes information. **Leaders in research and early education organize learning connections into "domains", that target the essential areas of learning for proper development and achievement: language, cognitive, physical, social & emotional.**

I have broken down these learning domains into eight simple "learning targets", for ease of understanding and implementation in a home setting. This is an easy way to think about how children learn, and how you can expose them each day to the things every growing child needs.

LANGUAGE
Let's Listen, Let's Talk
Let's Read, Let's Write

COGNITIVE
Let's Figure Things Out
Let's Pretend

PHYSICAL
Let's Use Our Hands
Let's Move Our Bodies

SOCIAL & EMOTIONAL
Let Me Be Me
Let's Be Friends

Understanding learning domains will empower you to know if your child is right on track, needs work in one area, or may require intervention (for example like a speech delay). I knew my middle daughter was progressing at a different rate than her siblings and was struggling with recognizing printed words. She was later diagnosed with dyslexia and dyscalculia, through my continued advocacy.

If a child is having difficulty putting sequences together or grouping  similar objects there may be an issue such as a learning disability or they may simply need direction or more practice. Being engaged in how her or she plays can help identify early issues and concerns. Often the earlier, the better.

Using these simple eight learning targets, you can make sure your child is exposed to all areas of learning daily and can facilitate what he or she needs. **Refer to Part III: How to Structure a Day**.

For example, an only child will have less social and emotional experience than a child with two siblings. It would be important to organize play dates or attend play groups to expose that child to social situations, especially before starting formal schooling. It will be less stressful for the child and he or she will feel much more confident interacting with other children and being with new adults.

Another example would be a child who is drawn to Legos and constantly asks or plays with them. It isn't necessary to deter that child from playing with Legos, but instead encourage and set up things that expose him or her to other learning areas, like reading, listening, or writing. If the resources are not available, a child will not grow in those necessary areas.

Note, that even though these connections are grouped into areas of a child's learning, a child learns in an integrated fashion.

Integrated learning means that more than one connection is

happening at a time. **One connection triggers another or affects another.** Areas of learning will overlap, and some activities will reach all learning connections and domains at once.

If a child plays a game of ball, for example, he or she will use more than one connection, and many connections simultaneously.

The child will...

1. **Call to another player** *(Language)*

2. **Follow instructions from his or her coach, or wait for a turn** *(Language, Cognitive, Social)*

3. **Use his or her hands and arms to catch and throw, and legs to run** *(Physical, Cognitive)*

4. **Talk before, during, and after the game with other players or his or her friends** *(Social/Emotional, Language)*

Even though a child appears to be participating in only one activity, many connections are happening at the same time.

Understanding these basics will give you the framework on how to facilitate situations and be creative in targeting learning domains in everyday life.

Learning areas will be integrated in a home environment.

LANGUAGE

Let's Listen, Let's Talk & Let's Read, Let's Write

Let's Listen, Let's Talk & Let's Read, Let's Write is the area of learning that refers to language and literacy development; the child's ability to understand and communicate the spoken and written language, in which he or she is immersed. Educators refer to this as receptive and expressive language.

A developing fetus is already constructing language through hearing and listening to its mother, and the sounds and people around her. These are the first experiences of receptive language and continues every time a child hears the spoken word.

Expressive language is the ability to speak or communicate. This progresses from crying, smiling, cooing, and babbling, to single words, a few words, then to sentences. Language is the most complex function of the brain. A child learns to express him or herself by learning from and using words they hear.

INDICATORS OF A CHILD'S PROGRESS THROUGH EARLY LANGUAGE DEVELOPMENT

RECEPTIVE LANGUAGE *(HEARING)*

- **Hears and distinguishes the sounds of words**
- **Recognizes sounds as letters and words** (phonetic)
- **Understands and follows two to four step directions**
- **Sits and pays attention to a story**

EXPRESSIVE LANGUAGE *(SPEAKING)*

- **Asks and answers relevant questions** (asks for juice or milk)
- **Recalls words in a song or rhyme**
- **Can tell or repeat a simple story**
- **Understands and figures out meaning from books** (non-fiction)
- **Uses words to express feelings and ideas**
- **Talks with other children during activities**
- **Makes up stories**
- **Speaks in increasingly complex sentences** (three to ten words)
- **Talks in a group** (more than two in a conversation)

LITERACY *(READING & WRITING)*

- **Enjoys and uses books appropriately** (opens front to back, turns pages)
- **Recognizes pictures and text on a page**
- **Understands the meaning of some print** (recognizes "STOP" on a top sign or the McDonald's arch)
- **Recognizes familiar words** (their name, "Dad," "dog")
- **Imitates by writing some letters, names, and numbers**
- **Makes increasingly representational drawings** (draws a face, a body, or a body with parts)

Let's Listen, Let's Talk Activity
Let's Read, Let's Write Activity
Tell an ABC story, sing the ABC song.
Trace the ABC's.

WHERE: Reading Area of Learning

TOOLS: ABC book

HOW: Have the children sit on a cushion or an alphabet square. Pull up a small chair or sit on the floor in front of them. Hold the book pages facing outward so that each child can see the book and hear you. If only one or two children, they can also sit next to you or in your lap. Allow ample time to tell the story. Pause between turning the pages so that each child can "study" the pictures, the print, and ask questions.

Next, get a piece of paper and pencil, or a small dry erase writing board. Draw dotted lines for a letter, "A". Have each child practice tracing the dots of the letter. Start with capital letters then advance to lower case, and so on. Pick one letter each week or start with your child's name.

CHALLENGES: Ask the children open-ended questions about the story. "Open-ended"= Who, What, When, Where, and How. For exam-

ple, "What picture did you see with the letter 'F' (sounding it out as efff)?" Ask questions about the story and sing the ABC song (two or three times) at a slow pace with the children. Now, practice tracing the word.

COGNITIVE

Let's Figure Things Out, Let's Pretend

Let's Figure Things Out, Let's Pretend is the area of learning that refers to cognitive development; the psychology of thinking, and how children acquire, construct, and use their increasing knowledge.

For a child this involves reasoning, problem-solving, logical and symbolic thinking, memory, concentration, attention span, and the ability to understand concepts. For example, a stove is hot to touch, and so not for play, but used for cooking.

The techniques in this book focus on infancy to age eight, and how the toys and equipment will evolve and expand as a child ages. Toys will be exchanged and replaced with more challenging and complex toys. For example, a three-year-old will not be able to construct a small Lego kit but can play with extra-large Legos. Different sizes will be introduced at different ages. This is how knowledge builds, from piecing together large basic creations to creating small complex ones.

It is fascinating to witness children advance to the next level!

INDICATORS OF A CHILD'S PROGRESS THROUGH EARLY COGNITIVE DEVELOPMENT

REASONING AND PROBLEM SOLVING
CONCENTRATION AND ATTENTION SPAN

- **Is curious and has a desire to learn** (asks questions)
- **Has interest in exploring**
- **Observes and makes discoveries**
- **Uses planning skills** (socks before shoes)
- **Shows creativity and imagination** (scribbles a picture and names it)
- **Applies information and experience to a new situation** (burns hand and learns not to touch the stove again)
- **Persists at task** (ranging from five to fifteen minutes)

LOGICAL THINKING AND MEMORY

- **Classifies objects as the same and different** (two apples, one apple, one orange)
- **Sorts objects that are the same** (apples with apples)
- **Recalls a sequence of events** (1st, 2nd, 3rd)

- **Arranges objects in a series** (a line, a circle)
- **Recognizes patterns and can repeat them** (red/white, red/white)
- **Increases in awareness of cause and effect** (rain makes things wet)

ABILITY TO UNDERSTAND CONCEPTS

- **Make-believe a pretend role or situation** (pretend to be a dog or doctor)
- **Make-believe with objects** (a fireman with a hose or extinguisher, or use a box as a boat)
- **Can sustain pretend play with friends** (from parallel play to cooperative play)
- **Shows increasing awareness of time concepts** (now, later, tomorrow)
- **Understands space concepts** (here, there, home, school)
- **Makes and interprets representations** (drawing a house, building with blocks)

Let's Figure Things Out Activity
Close, Dip, Open Dip Activity

WHERE: Art Area or Writing Area of Learning

TOOLS: Eye dropper, food coloring, water, coffee filters

HOW: Recite or chant the words, "Close, Dip, Open, Dip" each time you use the eye dropper to color the coffee filter. Saying or singing the words helps children to remember how to use the eye dropper.

CHALLENGES: Children can spend a lot of time working at this. Offer different kinds of paper, such as newspaper or construction paper, cut the paper into different shapes, or even just use paper towels. Ask where and how the colored water works best? Allow their work to dry. Then another day, let them paste their work into a collage, or just feel how each is different.

Let's Pretend Activity
Learning How-to Put-on Gloves

WHERE: House Area of Learning

TOOLS: Different sizes and types of unmatched gloves (children and adults size)

HOW: Have a variety of old winter mittens, mismatched single gloves, or yard gloves for dress up. Let the children practice putting them on and off.

This is not an easy task for little fingers! But when they need to wear mittens or gloves for outdoors, they will feel quite accomplished and competent that they are able to do it themselves!

CHALLENGES: After putting the gloves on successfully, sing, "Where Is Thumbkin?" to the tune of "Frère Jacques."

1. **Begin with two fists behind the back.** "Where is thumbkin? Where is thumbkin?"

2. **Bring out one fist with thumb raised.** "Here I am!"

3. **Bring out the other fist with thumb raised.** "Here I am!"

4. **Bend one thumb up and down.** "How are you today, sir?"

5. **Bend the other thumb up and down.** "Very well, I thank you!"

6. **Return one hand behind the back.** "Run away!"

7. **Return the other thumb behind the back.** "Run away!"

8. **Repeat with each finger (pointer, tallman, ring finer, pinkie).**

9. **Bring both hands, one at a time, with all fingers and thumbs raised, from behind the back.** End with, "Where is family?"

Children love to hear ryhmes and songs.

PHYSICAL

Let's Use Our Hands, Let's Move Our Body

Let's Use Our Hands, Let's Move Our Body is the area of learning that refers to a child's physical growth; Gross motor (large muscles), Fine motor (small muscles), Motor Skills development (increasing control over body and bodily functions), and the development of the five senses.

A child's physical growth is monitored by a pediatrician with regular physical exams beginning at birth. A child is asked to perform certain tasks

at the doctor's office, which inform the pediatrician of the normal range of the child's growth, gross and fine motor skills.

A child will progress from being asked if he or she knows who Mommy is, to if he or she can say "Mommy," to write his or her name, tie his or her shoes, hop on one foot, brush his or her teeth, and so forth. All these are general indicators of typical and proper development.

When a child enters formal schooling, the "tests" become more specific and these screenings reveal where your child stands in a developmental range.

INDICATORS OF A CHILD'S PROGRESS THROUGH EARLY PHYSICAL DEVELOPMENT

GROSS OR LARGE MUSCLE

- **Sits, crawls, stands walks**
- **Walks up and down steps with alternating feet**
- **Hops on two feet to hops on one foot**
- **Runs with increasing control over direction and speed**
- **Climbs up or down equipment without falling**
- **Pumps on a swing**
- **Skips**
- **Tumbles**
- **Jumps over and from objects without falling**
- **Catches and throws with aim**
- **Pedals and steers a tricycle**
- **Can perform proper jumping jacks**
- **Uses large muscles for balance** (walks in a straight line, stand on one foot or tiptoes)

FINE MOTOR OR SMALL MUSCLE

- **Handedness** (dominant hand left or right)
- **Grips** (with fists or fingers)
- **Coordinates eye-hand movement** (uses objects with control)

- **Hole punches**
- **Cuts with scissors**
- **Folds**
- **Self-help skills** (ties, zips, buttons)
- **Uses writing/drawing tools with increasing intention**
- **Prints letters & numbers**

THE FIVE SENSES
A child is able to identify...

- **Sounds** (a cat's meow, bell, wind)
- **Visual cues** (yellow is yellow, green means go)
- **Taste and smell** (sweet, sour)
- **Difference in texture** (rough, smooth)

Let's Use Our Hands Activity
Using Bingo Daubers

WHERE: Art Area or Writing Area of Learning

TOOLS: Paper pad or sheets, non-toxic bingo daubers (*these can be found at general pharmacies such as CVS or craft stores*)

HOW: Show the children how to unscrew and re-screw the caps on the bingo daubers. Explain that putting the cap back on will make them last longer (like markers) and they will not dry out. Explain that less air keeps them wet inside.

Give them a plain sheet of paper or cut the paper into different shapes and start "daubing". Say or chant slowly "Daub-a-Daub Daub, Daub-a-Daub Daub".

The repetition will help them to remember the action with words. Draging the dauber like a pencil or a marker will tear the dauber sponge.

The Dr. Seuss books about spots, "Put Me in the Zoo", "I Want to Be Somebody New", or "New Tricks I Can Do", by Robert Lopshire go well with this activity!

CHALLENGES: Draw shapes (circle, square, triangle, rectangle, or other) with a pen or pencil. Cut the paper into shapes or animals for spot decorating (like a Cheetah in the Dr. Seuss stories). Have the children "Daub-a-Daub Daub" on the lines, or inside the lines. While exercising their hands, they will also learn the names of shapes!

Let's Move our Bodies Activity
Walking a Line or a Balance Beam

WHERE: Climbing & Movement Area or Outdoor Area

TOOLS: Balance beam, flat board, or piece of wood, or ten to twelve-inches of painters' tape or masking tape (on the ground or floor)

HOW: Have the children walk across the board or line, one at a time. Ask the children if they want to hold your hand until they feel safe. After the first few "trips" across, elevate the board with blocks.

CHALLENGES: Have the children cross the beam or tape sideway. Next, have them repeat the activity on their tiptoes, and then on their heels. Older children can usually walk backwards, so encourage them to try. Have them do so on the balance beam if it can be done safely.

Change the masking tape into a zigzag, snake, or different geometric shapes to make the activity more challenging. I often did these activities outside in the driveway with chalk.

Leave this setup for a few days so the children can practice and master this activity! Also draw different lines to make roads. Use with a collection of cars or truck from the Construction & Block Area, or draw bigger roads to ride tricycles and scooters on! **Refer to Part I-II: Role of Facilitator.**

Social & Emotional

Let Me Be Me, Let's Be Friends

Let Me Be Me, Let's Be Friends is the area of learning that refers to healthy emotional and social development. This area is the heart of a child's ability to learn.

When a child feels emotionally secure and confident, a child is receptive to learning. As adults, we know it is difficult to concentrate in a state of stress if there has been a fight with a significant other or a job loss. If there is something bothering us it can be difficult to make it through the day.

Children are affected in the same way. It may be hearing Mommy and Daddy argue, having a fight with a sibling or friend, they are tired, or simply having a hard day. It is important to recognize children experience emotions as adults do. Social and emotional development touch two areas, the ability to develop social connections and emotional ones.

SOCIAL CONNECTION is a child's ability to get along with others, and to make friends. This is the ability to find their own identity, navigate relationships, and understand what is right from wrong.

EMOTIONAL CONNECTION is a child's ability to experience positive feelings of understanding, empathy, have self-esteem, and to express emotions (such as love, hate, anger, sadness, and loneliness), in a positive and socially acceptable way.

INDICATORS OF A CHILD'S PROGRESS THROUGH EARLY SOCIAL & EMOTIONAL DEVELOPMENT

EMOTIONAL

- **Is able to separate from parents**
- **Shows trust in other adults** (allows another adult to feed them)

- **Adapts to new situations** (stays without angst with a relative or babysitter)
- **Recognizes own feelings** (asks for a hug)
- **Recognizes feelings in others** (offers a hug)

- **Feels confident in growing abilities** (says "I did it myself")
- **Asserts self** (stands up for his or her rights)
- **Seeks help when needed** (asks for help cutting out a picture)
- **Capable of independent decision making**
- **Assumes responsibility for self** (puts on or takes off his or her own jacket)

SOCIAL

- **Identifies as a member of a family or culture**
- **Shows pride in heritage or background**
- **Seeks out other children and adults**
- **Shares toys and materials with others**
- **Respects boundaries; property and rights of others**

- **Follows routines** (brushes teeth before bed)
- **Respects rules by following them**
- **Plays and works well with other children** (says, "You can use my toy")
- **Thinks through and discusses conflict with others** (asks, "Give me back my toy, please!")

Let Me Be Me Activity
Working with Manipulatives

WHERE: Center Activity Table or Writing Area of Learning

TOOLS: Three manipulatives (Legos, puzzle, stackable magnets)

HOW: Set out three different manipulatives. If there is more than one child there should be enough resources so that each child can choose one without fighting. For a list of manipulatives **refer to PART I-II: Open Ended Toys & Open-Ended Toy Suggestions**.

CHALLENGES: Allow the children plenty of time to choose and explore each activity that is setup. Let the children struggle through trial and error before helping. If they are struggling put one piece in the right place, or guide them to try turning the piece around. Children will eventually become very capable, and this is part of figuring things out.

Once they have mastered an object you will see them begin to use their imaginations in what they do with them (for example building different towers with magnets). My children have built more structures than I ever could have imagined, and each time they were different!

For **LEGO MASTERS**, introduce small-size Legos and Lego kits as their fingers become more skilled. There are many different options. I began with extra-large ones until the choking hazard phase passed, and then introduced the next level when appropriate (large sized, to medium, then small).

For **PUZZLE MASTERS**, introduce a variety of puzzles with more pieces to increase the complexity level as they master easier ones. I started with the basic wooden puzzles of 4 to 5 pieces, increased to large floor puzzles and 20 to 40 pieces, and eventually progressed to small 100 plus piece puzzles.

Let's Be Friends Activity
How to Take Turns & Timers

WHERE: Any Learning Area

TOOLS: Face Clock (Analog), Timer, or a Stove Timer

HOW: Show the children the minute hand on the face of a clock. Tell them the "game" is to take turns! The first child will get at least ten minutes with a toy object (or longer depending on the ages of the children).

After ten minutes the other child will have a turn. Explain and show the hands and numbers on the clock. When the long hand gets to the "5", for example, it is the other person's turn to have the toy.

Put a sticker next to the number so the children will have a visual marker for when the time is up. You may be surprised when both children watch the clock and forget about the toy!

You can also use a minute timer that buzzes or rings, but this does not give the children as much chance or power to see time moving, and to begin to understand the concept of time.

CHALLENGES: Ask one child to be the timekeeper. Even very young children can learn to recognize numbers. Incorporating "real life" things into play, like using clocks, helps them understand in a fun way the world around them.

Time is a concept that can be understood even before a child can read time. Children learn there is a purpose to clocks and time, why we leave when we do, and sometimes why we rush. This is also a great activity to make taking turns fun (especially with siblings).

PART I-II

THE PLAYROOM

Defining and Choosing the Space

If you do not have an extra room, splitting a room in half also works, such as a living room, or you can set up different learning areas in different places. Each space just needs to be clearly defined so children know what to expect in those areas and what to do. They will begin to know that those areas are important, and to be used every day (writing, reading, listening, movement, and more).

If you choose a dedicated room it should be "theirs", where the rules are "different". In their space they can dump out toy, drop things, throw things, spill, tumble, fall safely, and more, without getting hurt or in trouble. I chose my dining room. I realized using my dining room twice a year for holidays was less important than establishing a dedicated place for my children to use every day.

For full time play areas, basements are not ideal. I do have a play area and toys in the basement (even now), but using the space solely as your play area means that children are generally out of sight, and most do not like to play alone. Until mine were close to double digits, they would ask me to go into the basement with them.

Whatever area you do decide, having it close to or part of the main living area is a much better option than a bedroom that is upstairs or down the hall, out of sight. A child needs to feel he or she is a part of what is going on, and will require less attention while you are cooking dinner, or when the other parent comes home from work, if the child is close to you and can see you. The child will feel a part of the unit even if playing alone.

Leaving a child unattended, even in a safe environment, can cause anxiety, stress, and fear. This is not conducive to play, let alone healthy development.

Many parents experience this separation anxiety when a child is left alone with a babysitter or start preschool for the first time.

When the play area is in or near the main living area, you can still engage with them, answer questions, listen to their stories, get them a drink of water, and give suggestions. Children are social beings. They want to be seen, heard, acknowledged, and recognized.

I purchased two large gates to block the large openings of my dining room. One side was open to the foyer while the other had French doors adjoining the kitchen. I did not want to have to close the doors. I wanted the space open so I could see and engage with my children, even if I was working in the kitchen.

Children need boundaries. Healthy boundaries begin with space. Gates defined our space. I could leave the gates open for supervised exploring or close them when I needed to check an email or make a phone call. The children were in a safe, fun place, and they knew it too.

I only removed the gates when my youngest was in second grade. Even before this, they learned to open and close the gates themselves, but they were old enough by that point that I let them manage the space.

When they are small, they are dependent on us. We feed them, pick them up, help them dress, wash, herd them into safety, buckle them into their seats, and so on. But as part of healthy development and growth, a child transitions to being the boss of his or her own body, and realizes he or she is ultimately in control of what happens to him or her.

Early on in life, every child needs a "secure base" and later a child needs a "framework" around him. Only when he feels securely anchored and contained will a child be able to follow rules consistently."
-Dr. Michael Thompson, How to Raise Responsible Children

Many children are left in play pens for long periods of time. This not only hinders physical development but most other areas of development as well. Play pens can be used for naps, short rest times, travel, or less than thirty minutes at a time.

As my children started walking and needing more daily physical activity, I set up different activities for them in different parts of the house to encourage exploration and curiosity, as well as movement. This would break up the boredom of being in one room (even if the activities were temporary).

I also set out puzzles and games at the kitchen table or counter, where we would work together. This was dedicated, structured, quality time together. **Refer to Part I-II: Structured Toys and Part III: How to Structure a Day.**

Setting up the Room, the Basics

To small children, the world feels very big. This is why we create learning areas and set up play spaces just their size.

Everything in the playroom should be usable and within reach for a child.

Things should be child-sized (other than universal items like measuring cups or plastic Tupperware containers), that can be used at any age. Even scissors come in different sizes because a child's small hands cannot operate adult-size ones!

Safety!
Suggestions & Recommendations

Safety is an important consideration. Some of these may be common sense, but when I emptied my dining room, I wanted a place where I could leave my baby to crawl or toddler to toddle, and explore safely. As they got older, they could climb and use anything in the playroom they wanted. It was their space.

1. Electrical outlets are covered, and cords removed.

2. Toys are age appropriate. Check for choking hazards, things that could break easily, glass, or hard objects.

3. Floor is covered with a rug or soft materials in case a child falls, especially a toddler. I had two rugs and purchased a soft alphabet mat with letters. It also served as a puzzle for curious toddlers.

4. Windows are closed and locked. In summer if you have open screens make sure to have window guards. A child does not realize if they push on a screen they could fall through and get hurt.

5. Equipment is secure and cannot be pulled down on a child. Some kitchens or dollhouses may need to be secured to the wall. Televisions are another feature in a split room that could be pulled down on top of a child. Anything heavy should be properly mounted to the wall.

Organization & Storage

Containers and bins for toys are an integral part of being able to manage the space. **Toys that are not being used should be out of sight and out of mind!** I was always amazed when my children would play with something as if it was completely new when it had only been put away for a week or so. They played with the same toys for years but each time they were rotated in they were like new.

Of course, when they were older and taller, they could access every-thing themselves, but when they were younger, most toys were out of reach. Also, if you have older children who play with more complex toys, putting those toys away and out of reach when not in use establishes a safe zone for younger siblings (as some toys cannot be played with unsupervised due to choking hazards).

I had a mudroom with cabinets where I kept most of our puzzles, manipulatives, games, and arts and crafts. I also used the top shelf of a closet and the high shelf in the washer and dryer area for larger options (like the various toy play houses I had). Once these were organized, rotating toys became simple and easy.

Extra cabinets in the kitchen, the basement, or closets in other rooms also work. Even the garage is a great storage space, although toys can get chilly to the touch in colder months. Just make sure the equipment is easily accessible and kept in closed containers if outside (so moisture and critters can't get inside and ruin the toys).

There are many storage options on the market. I purchased various stackable and clear bins. This made storing toys and games easy. I discovered the perfect size was a standard shoebox size. This size fit most activities and toy sets perfectly (such as our collection of dinosaurs, army soldiers, sea creatures, people for the farmhouse, stackable cups, magnets, Legos, and so on).

Larger bins will be needed for larger sets and as you continue to add more toys to your collections. Many things will be added over time, like play dough tools, cars, dolls, houses accessories, action figures, and more. I did not bother to label the bins because it was easier during cleanup to just throw an activity into whichever bin was empty or closest.

I couldn't always see what was in the bins in the cabinets, but my routine was to pull out four to five each morning to set up. Imagine cabinets full of bins stacked on top of each other; that is what I had. Even though some toys had been changed or replaced over the years, the system works! Being organized is essential for rotating toys easily. Find a system that works for you.

Types of Toys & Equipment

There are many different options, variations, and types of toys. Some toys are used one time or played with for a short time, and never again (a birthday or holiday present). Many become dust collectors on a shelf or sit at the bottom of a toy box. Unfortunately, many things offered in the toy industry are not only expensive but useless long term. A toddler will often spend more time with an empty box and packaging than a toy itself.

Sometimes a box of plain sticks and buttons are a better option that an expensive toy, and can keep children entertained for close to an hour. All toys are not created equal.

By recognizing and providing the right toys you can facilitate learning just by offering them, and the right toys can be used for years. The type of play will evolve as your children grow.

For example, while playing with blocks, a toddler will first simply explore the different types of objects. They will start by touching, biting, feeling, holding, carrying, and throwing them (sensory development). This play will then progress to stacking, sorting, making towers, and knocking the blocks down. The play will then evolve to building different types of structures, and eventually to using the blocks in complex and dramatic play; building structures and playing with them, buildng a city, then building with a friend or friends, to hosting a group dinosaur invasion.

I personally dislike stuffed animals. They tend to collect dust and are horrible for children with allergies. But, a stuffed animal is great to cud-

dle and feel, and often becomes a favorite transitional toy. Children do see them as "friends" and absolutely love how cute and cuddly they are. They are an unavoidable part of childhood. And when children are given other resources, stuffed animals are great when playing veterinarian or as an audience to a puppet show.

By investing in the right toys a parent can facilitate learning that lasts for years! **The right use of toys can build a solid foundation of knowledge!**

Open-Ended Toys

Open-ended toys are some of the greatest toys. They have endless possibilities. A child can use his or her imagination to create and experiment. Every time a child uses an open-ended toy, he or she can create something different or the toy can be used in a variety of ways (Legos, dress-up clothes, blocks, musical instruments).

These types of toys also save a lot of money because they can be used repeatedly, for years, at all different ages and stages of development.

Children's small hands are comfortable and attracted to something that can be touched, used, taken apart, and put back together over and over again.

A common open-ended toy is called a manipulative. **A manipulative is an object that is designed for a child to learn by "manipulating" it.**

While playing with manipulatives, a child learns concepts such as counting, stacking, sorting and deconstructing, matching, construction, patterning, categorizing, and comparing (building blocks of math). **Manipulatives help develop and enhance fine motor skills and hand-eye coordination.** They help a child learn about measurable concepts like shapes, numbers, and symbols, in a hands-on and experimental way.

Manipulatives are objects like textured links, sorting shapes, blocks, rings, balls, puzzles, or stacking toys. These are perfect for every day play or

just to dump in the tub during bath time for water play.

Other open-ended toys are action figures, figurines, playhouses, play money, farm animals, trucks, playdough accessories, dinosaurs, and more.

A small work bench with toy-drills, saws, wood pieces, and screws for construction are great to rotate in and out.

I also had a dual-combination board that had one side for magnets and the other side for felt board stories.

The magnet board can be used with magnets to teach animals, shapes, objects, or with dry erase markers to teach letters or words. Felt board stories are a great alternative to reading books. **Refer to Part III: Reading Area.** Children will also use the magnet and felt board pieces like figurines in pretend play.

When my children started understanding the concept of money and how money was used to pay for things, I bought play money, a working cash register, and calculators. Making your own money is also easy and super fun. These were added to the House Area of Learning and added an entirely new level to playing "store". **Refer to Part III: House Area, Additional Options, Playing Store.** For one Christmas each of my children got a package of labels in their stockings! Everything in the entire playroom ended up with price tags (even people).

Open-Ended Toys Suggestions

INFANTS & TODDLERS

- **Play kitchen with pretend food**
- **Stacking cubes**
- **Baby dolls**
- **Wooden blocks**
- **Mr. Potato Head**

PRESCHOOLERS

- **Toy trains, tracks, cars, and trucks**
- **Blocks, Magnet Tiles**
- **Role-playing kits** (doctor, veterinarian, other)
- **Dress-up clothes** (costumes, simple pieces of materials)
- **Magnetic letters & numbers**
- **Pegs & peg boards**
- **Interlocking links & cubes**
- **Felt board and felt board story pieces**
- **Matching games** (start with colors or pictures to matching and making words)
- **Puppets and other story telling materials**

ELEMENTARY-AGE CHILDREN

- **Dolls & dollhouse**
- **Action & Superhero figures**
- **Legos**
- **Dominoes**
- **Card games**
- **Board games**
- **Make-believe** (school or house)
- **Military toys**

Structured Toys

Structured toys have a clear beginning, middle, and end. Structured toys can only be put together one way and are self-correcting. There is generally a rule or set of rules, and each piece plays a clear role in the completion of the play activity (such as puzzles or nesting blocks). The materials themselves indicate the method of play.

An example is a sequencing word game that uses three letters to make a word, like C-A-T. Together the letters form a picture of a cat, which is easier for young children to put together. As the puzzle is completed by forming the picture, the child will start to recognize the pattern and associate the letters to the word, and eventually learn to spell CAT. Not only has the child solved a problem toward mastery and independence, but he or she is beginning to memorize concepts, as well as to understand sequencing and consequence.

These types of toys evolve as a child develops. More difficult activities, games, and puzzles will be needed as a child masters easier ones.

Structured Toy Suggestions

INFANTS & TODDLERS
- **Ring stackers**
- **Empty containers**
- **Stacking cups**
- **Shape sorter**
- **Graduated cups** (measuring cups that fit together)
- **Inset puzzles** (a single piece fits in a single space in a board, often wooden puzzles with knobs in the shape of farm animals or people)
- **Puzzles** (one to five large pieces)

PRESCHOOLERS
- **Basic board games** (Bingo, Candyland, Chutes & Ladders)
- **Floor puzzles** (ten to thirty pieces)
- **Building blocks**
- **Lacing cards** (thread holes with yarn or string, or sewing cards)
- **Peg boards with a set number of pegs**
- **Puzzles** (ten to thirty pieces)

ELEMENTARY-AGE CHILDREN
- **Board games for older children** (pictionary, hangman)
- **Model vehicle sets** (trucks, cars, airplanes)
- **Puzzles** (thirty to fifty pieces)
- **Lego kits/sets**
- **Engineering design & building kits**

Creating Collections

Establishing collections of toys will lead to years of inventive and creative play. With a collection of toys, a child can create his or her own world of battles, challenges, rescues, and more.

A child may express interest in "army guys", so one or two are purchased. But if there is only one or two, there is not much else to do with them. However, if these same army guys are added to a collection of superheroes, or a collection of army guys with different colors, trucks, equipment  and tools, the play becomes much more complex. The imaginative and pretend play scenarios become infinite.

Each time a new character is added or an accessory to a collection, it adds an entirely new element, and a brand new play scenario will unfold!

I had many types of collections and added to them over time, such as different types of magnet creatures, figurines, houses, and more. Many of these toys you may already have.

 Once my children were older and past putting toys in their mouth and the choking phase, I even bought cheap items from the dollar stores to add to our collections. You can never have enough playdough tools or bugs in a bug collection.

Collections of Toys Suggestions

- **Play houses, figurines, accessories**
- **Action figures, superheroes**
- **Service heroes** (police, fire, ambulance, doctors, other)
- **Various food sets**
- **Military & accessories** (army soldiers, navy sailors, military trucks, barracks, hills, fences, other)
- **Vehicles & accessories** (cars, tracks, garages, monster trucks, road signs, other)

- **Dolls & Dollhouses** (clothes and house accessories)
- **Shopkin houses, accessories**
- **Babies or life-size dolls, clothes, accessories**
- **Puzzles** (wooden, floor puzzles, Jigsaw puzzles)
- **Dinosaurs, environmental accessories**
- **Farm** (animals, equipment, barn/farmhouse, accessories, other)
- **Sea Creatures** (types of whales, fish, sharks, other)
- **Bugs & Creatures**
- **Magnet Board & Magnets**
- **Blocks**
- **Felt Board and Felt board stories**
- **Playdough & Sand accessories**
- **Other**

Playroom Guidelines

Guidelines and rules need to be established, not only for your children, but also for guests. I made sure anyone who played at our house or in our playroom knew the rules. Everyone who played was expected to follow them, even adults. There is much less fighting over toys when the rules are the same for everyone. It sounds simple enough but many families have different rules and this can cause unnecessary angst.

It is often difficult for children to have friends come into their space as they see everything as their own. Sharing and following the rules of engagement is one of the hardest transitions for children when they begin school. Understanding rules early help ease this process.

SUGGESTIONS FOR PLAYROOM RULES IN A HOME OF LEARNING

1. Define the rules. It is never too early to begin. Babies may not understand complex sentences, but they do understand facial expressions and changes in tone of voice. "No", is also one of the most often-used words a growing child hears. That's why having a playroom with only a few of them is so powerful.

2. Explain and make sure the rules are understood. Review them as necessary; they will need to be repeated. Many of the rules are common and will be the same on play dates or in school.

3. Provide enough materials and equipment. If you have more than three children in a space, you may need two of certain items (two sets of stacking cups or paint brushes).

4. Always check to make sure equipment is clean and safe. Remove any broken toys or pieces, and clean regularly.

5. All activities require adult supervision, guidance, some participation, and continuous involvement.

6. Children should never be left unattended and unsupervised. Young children should always be in sight. My mantra is, "I need to see you or hear you," especially when we are in public places. Active children do not want to stay in a carriage or stroller. As they got older, I let them run or walk free as long as they were in my line of sight, or I could hear them close by.

7. Rotate the toys! Change the materials and toys regularly. Each time a toy is taken out of storage it feels like new! If the children seem bored or do not play with what is out, it may be your cue to change or increase the level of complexity.

8. Toys in the playroom are for everyone in the room and to be shared. This includes brothers, sisters, moms, dads, relatives, and friends.

9. If someone is playing with a toy, ask if you can have a turn. If the person does not want to share, then you will have to wait, and turns will be taken. Refer to PART I: Let's Be Friends Activity, How to Take Turns & Timers.
A child quickly knows when things are fair and will respect and appreciate it (even in the terrible two's and three's), as long as the rules are consistently enforced. I still adhere to this rule, if they cannot agree to take turns or teasing starts, I simply take it away.

10. Special toys are special toys and do not need to be shared. Everyone knows what those toys are, and the rule is the same for everyone. These are not to be touched unless permission is granted.
In my house, it was a teddy bear for my oldest, a snuggle lamb blanket for my middle child, and a snuggle bear blanket for my youngest. These are

often referred to as transitional objects. My "special toy" was my cell phone.

Toys such as birthday presents or Christmas gifts that a child does not want to share also do not need to be shared, but toys in the playroom are for everyone and they are to be shared.

This rule became more important as my children got older and realized they didn't want to share everything, and began to have their own interests and hobbies. My son kept his "Army trucks" in his room, my middle child kept her "Shopkins", and my oldest kept her "Uglies". When they wanted someone to play with, they invited them into their room, or brought these toys into the playroom.

This rule supports the idea of boundaries and independence, but also encourages social and emotional development. This tends to be the area most children struggle with when they start school.

11. No hitting or throwing toys.

12. If the rules are not followed there should be a logical consequence (one that makes sense to a child, unlike spankings). I used timeouts, to take place outside of the playroom (a break from play). I had a dedicated chair right next to the playroom. *A good rule for time is one minute per age maximum.* If they get up from the timeout (as very young children won't sit long and are more likely to get up), keep putting them back in the chair without saying a word. I always explained why. For instance, "Hitting Sara is not okay. You have to sit here." Set a timer. I would make it less about the actual time, and instead, not let them out until they were ready to explain why they were in timeout.

Ask, "Why did Mommy put you in timeout?" At the beginning, many times they will not want to admit why because they feel guilty about what they did. They do not want to disappoint you or make you upset. But this step teaches consequences and makes them take responsibility, for example if they hit someone else. I also made sure to thank them after they admitted what they did, gave them a big hug, told them I was proud of them, and loved them. Then we resumed normal activities.

Children not only need physical boundaries but emotional ones as well.

Children learn by observing what we do. Many children with behavioral problems suffer because they do not understand healthy boundaries. They hit, take things that do not belong to them, do not want to share, and do not follow rules.

Even though true independence is a slow transition as a child grows, teaching a child he or she is responsible for his or her actions should happen as soon as he or she understands words. This empowers them to make choices and realize what they do matters. We want to teach a child that he or she is boss of his or her own body and that he or she is in control of what happens to it.

13. "No" means "No". After going through this many times with my children, I find it easier to say no firmly and not waver in my decision. If they are misbehaving with a toy, for example, simply say, "Stop or I will take it away." If they do not stop, take it away. No threats. No anger. No negotiation. When they cry, reassert the reason, "I told you when you do 'this,' I will take the toy away." This is cause and effect.

This not only teaches consequence, but it also puts the power and choice in the child's hand. Explaining why is critical in their understanding. Getting mad or taking it away without reason does not teach them cause and effect, or why. Testing you is how they learn boundaries. Defiance is often less about behaving badly than it is about learning and experimenting with social and emotional boundaries.

The power struggle is certainly one of the hardest times as a parent because it can feel daunting and overwhelming, but it does pass. The real challenge is to be consistent, strong, understanding, and loving all at the same time. Easy right? In the end, it is just feelings, and they are trying to figure out what to do with them.

Believe it or not, these behavioral issues show that your child has a strong bond with you and the confidence to find his or her own self. They trust they can be who they are, and you will still be there and love them. These behaviors are testing grounds for what they can and cannot do, often with feelings they are experiencing and navigating for the first time.

Preparedness

Preparedness is important for a child. In this context, I mean explaining to your child or children what is happening now, and what will happen next. This ties directly into transition time. **Preparing your child mentally for what is expected in advance allows them to "prepare" themselves.**

Children live in the moment. They are not looking at the clock. They do not understand when they need to leave in fifteen minutes, or why it is important. They are preoccupied with whatever task they are doing at that moment, in the moment, playing with a toy or getting dressed.

I try to always tell my children what is happening next and why, especially in sequence, which seems simple enough, but so often as parents we forget to communicate with our children. We are often too busy rush-

ing around. Then we wonder why our children are acting up, not prepared to leave, or giving us a hard time.

For example, if we are in the car and almost home, I say, "When we get home, I want you to go inside and get your pajamas on. Then we are going to have a snack and do homework." So, when we get inside and I tell them again to get their pajamas on, now they are prepared and know what is expected. I also try to let them know when things will be out of schedule in advance, such as, "Today we have to go to the doctor's office right after school for your sister's checkup, so we won't have time to play after you get off the bus." In explaining and communicating, we are constantly teaching them.

Another great example is getting to school on time. I say, "Everyone has to get to school at the same time because otherwise it would be chaos and there would be consequences. What if everyone in your class got to school at different times? How would the teacher know what and when to teach?"

It makes sense. Life goes much smoother and easier when children are pre-pared and know what to expect and are engaged in the process, rather than simply herded like sheep (although we all have been in that position too).

Preparedness establishes confidence and trust. Children learn what you say happens and to trust your word. This carries into every facet of life, from why they need to brush their teeth, to when it's time to go to sleep. Not only does talking to and with children help with cognition, planning, and language development, it also creates great listeners.

Transition Time

Transition time is the time it takes for a child to "adjust" to a new circumstance or situation. Children need transition time between events, tasks, and even normal day to day activities (before a movie, after a movie, before leaving for school, after getting home, before going to bed, after getting up from bed, and so on). Transitions go on and on. It's almost as

if children store pent up energy that needs to be expelled before they can settle into another task. Their brains need to reset.

Ask any schoolteacher or early childcare provider; they will attest to this collective time between one activity and the next. This time is often over-looked as we try to get them to do their homework, take a shower, or even sit down for a meal, and it often ends in frustration and anxiety.

Transition time doesn't have to be long, but naturally built into a child's day. Simply build in an extra ten minutes (for example, before leaving for school). Give a ten-minute warning, then a five-minute warning, then a time to go warning. It works!

Doing this not only makes life as a parent easier but it also allows the child the necessary time to release energy, and mentally and physically prepare for the next thing. Transition time is a natural and necessary thing every child needs.

The Role of Facilitator

The role of facilitator is a very important and powerful role that everyone who cares for a child has.

Facilitator: One that facilitates, one that helps to bring about an outcome (as learning, productivity, or communication) by providing indirect or unobtrusive assistance, guidance, or supervision - Merriam-Webster Dictionary

The goal of this book is to empower you as a facilitator, to create a positive and enriched environment (with proper resources and circumstances for enhanced learning and development), and to provide support along the way as your child grows.

Many parents believe they are doing "facilitation" right, providing play dates, sending the child to preschool, signing them up for soccer, even buying them the toys they want. While these are right ways to facilitate a child's life, without facilitating "learning", our opportunity as the greatest resource for our child can be missed.

Imagine giving an adult a bicycle who has never seen or ridden one, and not showing them how or what to do. The adult may be able to figure it out, but most likely, they would try, fall, and probably never ride again. A child, new to the world, is the same.

If you just give a child a cup, they will hold it for a minute then drop it. It is not because this cup does not have possibilities or use, it just holds no immediate purpose for the child. The child does not know the possibilities. However, if you create the proper setting and facilitate learning, giving this same child, a spoon, and a cup full of water, that minute will turn into five.

And if you give that same child a cup and spoon outside, a bucket of water, and a hose, the five minutes will turn into twenty, and so on. Rather than simple observation, the activity will turn into exploration and a rich, sensory integration experience.

To become a facilitator is to create possibilities and opportunities for learning right in your home, every day.

This is actually not more work. I felt like I had more free time because my children were occupied. I was not their sole source of entertainment. My children were busy while I was able to do other things. I also had the peace of mind knowing I was not just sticking them in front of a TV or on a device so I could have a break (even though I did that at times too).

Teaching also happens naturally in this type of rich learning environment. They will constantly ask for help and guidance, and they will engage you.

One day, for my son's preschool field trip we went for a hike in a local, well-maintained state forest. I ended up in a group with an affluent mother who refused to let her five-year-old daughter venture off a groomed path, even slightly into the woods. She didn't want her going too far, or tripping over a stick, and repeatedly told her to be careful or stay on the path. There were seven of us watching these kids. I, of course, let my son run ahead, into the woods, climb the rocks, find sticks, look for bugs, throw rocks, step in puddles, fall down, and more. I still don't understand what the mother was afraid would happen.

If her daughter fell and got a bruise or scraped her knee, that is part of growing and learning. She would heal, and probably learn better balance, to look before she ran, watch her step, or be aware of vines. The mother prevented her child from enjoying the sensory experience of being in the woods and touching and feeling the world around her.

Which child do you think would grow up strong and confident, if this was an everyday experience? Yet, I believe both of us wanted what was best for our child. The ever-popular term for this today is called a "helicopter parent".

The challenge in this scenario is the mother believed she was being a conscientious caretaker, keeping her child safe. But she missed her role as a facilitator.

My son started crawling in a playroom with climbing slides and structures where he wouldn't get hurt falling, exploring, and trying things on his own. He was not only physically stronger but more capable of running and climbing. The risks were less for him running free in the woods. He also knew his own boundaries, and he knew that if he went too far, he could lose sight of us. Putting the responsibility in his hands is part of being a facilitator.

If you can capitalize on the constant opportunity you have while a child plays, to create and facilitate learning, you can also become your child's greatest teacher.

Each night after the children went to sleep or before they woke up, I would clean the playroom and put all the toys away. I did a clean sweep of the space. All toys were put in their right places, and toys that were used on the Center Activity Table or rotated in, were put away. Out of sight, out of mind.

A clean space is a blank canvas for a child to create and become the master of his or her environment, even if to us, they just made a huge mess. Believe it or not, children do not like chaos. Children get overwhelmed when there is too much stimuli or too many options.

New parents learn this very quickly when they buy a colored, twelve-bin organizer with all the toys in different bins for a toddler. They soon find that all the toys end up in a pile on the floor in about five minutes. Dumping the toys out is more fun than playing with them and this is a normal part of development, cause and effect. Less is best.

Often the child does not know how to play with a toy until he or she see someone else playing with it, or an adult provides some guidance. **Facilitation is setting up learning in a way that a child can explore and discover, and if he or she needs guidance, you guide them.**

Putting the farm animals out with a farmhouse or barn, for example, and placing the animals in their proper spaces is facilitating learning. The cow

 is placed in the stall where the moo sound is made. A toddler will first pick up the cow, touch it, feel it, bite it, throw it, and walk away. There is no association to what it is or why, as of yet. Over time however, the child will learn what a cow is and what it does, play with the cow saying Moo, know where it fits in a farm, and that the milk they drink comes from a cow.

These are the building blocks of exploration, learning through play, and learning. This is why children need certain types of toys and guidance at different developmental stages to aid in this process of constructing knowledge.

As children get older, between two and four, you should no longer have to set up the animals in their proper places. Although coming downstairs in the morning and seeing all your toys set up waiting for you is like Christmas morning! I would often surprise my daughters by staging their dollhouse or my son's cars in a monster truck show, with one of his garages. Hours of play awaited. I tried to set up toys to give each child exposure to all areas of learning each day, and if one was missed, it would be covered the next day. I did not follow a strict schedule. Instead I let things flow and the routine came naturally.

Many toys overlap between one space and another. For example, the Melissa & Doug cutting board that had been set out on the Center Activity Table would often end up in the oven in the House Area of learning. All toys weave together, like a small little world for a child. **Refer to PART II: Center Activity Table and PART II: House Area.**

Once my children were in preschool two or three days a week, I often rotated the toys bi-weekly because their daily use was less. When they became of school age, they were old enough to choose the toys and activities themselves. However, on days there was no school and in the summer, I would continue to facilitate, or whenever they seem bored and needed a "jump start".

Do not feel like you must have everything, nor do you have to buy the same items I had. The goal is to understand the different types of toys, how to rotate in items that target learning domains, and how to facilitate learning! **Refer to PART III: Quick Guide: Rotations of Toys & Learning Areas and PART III: How to Structure a Day Suggestions.**

PART II

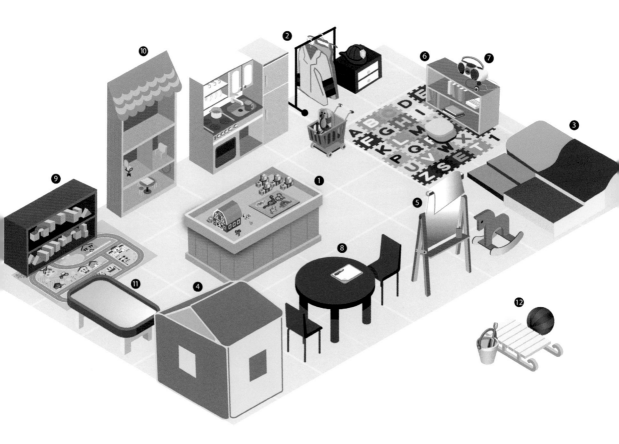

Play & Learning Areas in the Home

Part of the national standards for accredited early learning programs, by the National Association for the Education of Young Children (NAEYC), is to establish areas around a facility called "centers". **Centers target areas of learning and are dedicated to the learning domains of a developing child** (art, blocks, cooking, discovering science, dramatic play, literacy, math and manipulatives, music and movement, sand play, and water play). **Refer to Part I: Areas of Learning & Learning Connections.**

Centers are stationary, consistent, and structured areas for play. These areas are constantly re-equipped and follow a plan throughout the year (often with themes).

In a preschool setup, the materials and toys of centers are rotated in and out, and changed regularly. One month, the theme may be structured around service occupations. The dress-up clothes will be changed to doctors, police, firemen, or other. Play medical equipment will be put in the House/Dollhouse Center. A police officer or fire truck may do a day visit.

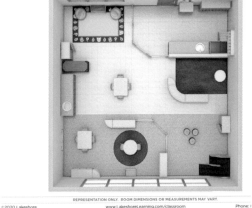

REPRESENTATION ONLY. ROOM DIMENSIONS OR MEASUREMENTS MAY VARY.

©2020 Lakeshore   www.LakeshoreLearning.com/classroom   Phone: 1

Instead of setting up all the centers (which would be difficult with limited space), I created one playroom and essentially combined the fundamental components of these centers into a smaller setting. I set up areas in the room I call "learning areas".

Learning areas are dedicated areas of play with pre-set equipment and materials, for children to choose and use throughout their day, and can accommodate multi-aged interests and abilities. My dining room was a great size for three small children. Most areas were stationary, like the Kitchen Area and Dollhouse Area of learning, where children could free play, but I also used the Center Activity Table to rotate toys and target learning areas within them.

From each preschool learning center, I identified specific equipment and toys that had the best application in a smaller setting. I also learned through trial and error which resources worked best to target the areas of learning in a free-play home environment. In a home setting, many learning areas over-lap and will be used by different ages (especially open-ended toys and manip-ulatives, **refer to PART I-II: Types of Toys & Equipment, Open-Ended Toys**), and for multiple purposes (the structures used in the Climbing Area of learning, for example, are often used for reading or playing, rather than climbing, **refer to PART II: Climbing & Movement Area)**.

Most adults do not realize that developing children work very hard when they play. Children use all their resources and energy to participate in and make sense of the world around them. Children learn when challenged by settings and tools that foster their growing skills and promote these skills and abilities. **Setting up learning areas enables a parent to effectively and strategically manage space to a child's benefit.**

The diagram of all the learning areas included can be deceiving. It does not require a large room. **These areas can be set up in different parts of the house or apartment, or even different corners of a room. The concept of learning areas is more about understanding different types**

 **of play and to create areas dedicated to it**, rather than having to establish a large area for equipment.

Depending on what age you begin, children between three and six will require more complex and rich play, than an infant up to two years old who will be more interested in shapes, colors, textures, sizes, and exploring toys. A six-month-old, for example, will not play with a cash register the same way a two-year-old would. And, it is not as useful or applicable as it will be for a five-year-old.

All items do not need to be purchased immediately or be in your play-room on the first day (especially if you only have a six-month-old). The basic learning areas should be established, but start with a few items as you set up, and add throughout the years: look for yard sales, families with older children getting rid of things (people are always outgrowing toys and love to donate them), or special events and occasions.

Once you get into a rhythm of what toys to acquire, adding to your home of learning will be easy and natural. As you walk through the toy store or stop at a yard sale, you will hone in on toys your children will learn from, and target things that will add to your set up. Children will outgrow some toys, but most will be used for years.

12 LEARNING AREAS

1. Center Activity Table
2. House Area
3. Climbing & Movement Area
4. Playhouse Area
5. Art Area
6. Reading Area
7. Listening Area
8. Writing Area
9. Construction & Block Area
10. Dollhouse Area
11. Sensory Table
12. Outdoor Area

Center Activity Table

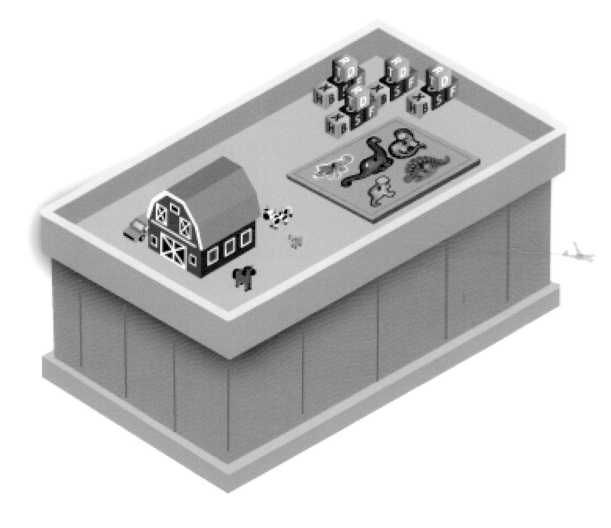

The Center Activity Table is "center stage" to rotate toys and activities. This sat in the center of my playroom (until my oldest turned thirteen)! The Center Activity Table usually hosts the main event.

After visiting a preschool, my nine, seven, and six-year old decided to play "daycare" taking care of our babies from the House Area of learning. The Center Activity Table became the the feeding and changing station. At one point my six-year-old son hopped on and pretended to be a baby himself, for attention from his sisters.

After my middle daughter's annual doctor visit, the Center Activity Table became the "examination room". She set up a bench for her medical equipment, the toy doctor kit, miscellaneous items, and her plastic "laptop". She learned this from her doctor who uses a laptop to type on while she asks questions. The nurse gave her some supplies before we left (latex gloves, depression sticks, swabs for cultures, gauze, and masks), so the playroom transformed into a "doctor's office" for over a week. My children became veterans at imaginative play and used the all the resources available, and The Center Activity Table was always an integral part.

THE TABLE: I used an old wooden table designed to hold train sets. When my children were babies and beginning to crawl the Center Activity Table was the perfect height to pull themselves up on and learn to stand. Having a table full of colorful objects is quite an incentive for any child to pull themselves up to explore. Eventually, they would toddle around the table, getting stronger and more stable, until they were walking.

The lip of the table is important for young children as it prevents toys from falling to the floor and creates a barrier for play. It seems like a simple design feature, but it truly serves an important function. The lip creates a boundary for small children and acts as a guide when building towers or lining up cars. It gives a framework for the houses to sit up against and

acts as a buffer (for balls, wheels, and more). It will prevent you and the children from having to constantly pick up pieces from the floor, and as the toys and pieces get smaller and more detailed. The lip helps pieces from being lost (like on a complicated model or Lego set). One

missing piece is frustrating! If you cannot find a table with a lip add one with thin pieces of molding from your local hardware store

Many stores sell different types of train tables, just make sure it is solid and big enough for children to climb on and use for many different scenarios. Some tables are too short, and the children quickly outgrow them, leading them to bend over uncomfortably to play. I found the ideal height was seventeen inches tall. .

CENTER ACTIVITY TABLE ACTIVITIES: On the Center Activity Table, each day, put out a variety of options of open-ended toys and structured toys. Each day I would try to put out one game, a few puzzles, three to five manipulatives (magnetic or alphabet blocks), one playhouse or garage, and one collection of figures (people or farm animals and accessories; vehicles and miscellaneous items). If you have more than one child, mix the toys based on developmental level (for example, puzzles appropriate for each age). Some days, I would put out five puzzles and one manipulative, the dinosaurs and volcano pieces, a mat, and trees instead of a playhouse.

PUZZLES & MANIPULATIVES: Having many age appropriate puzzles and manipulatives are the simplest way to keep children engaged and learning. Learning is so much more than being able to complete a task; it is figuring, practicing, building, creating, anticipating, and trying. Open-ended and structured toys help children gain know-how. Doing a puzzle not only requires dedication and attention, it teaches and requires a child to practice planning, coordination, patience, problem solving, spatial reasoning, and more.

Typically, if your children are very young (ten-months to three-years-old), all toys will require some level of introduction and facilitation. **Refer to Part I-II: The Role of Facilitator.** Some children may breeze through activities and puzzles in fifteen minutes and need more options. Some children may take longer.

When my son was between three and four years old, I introduced a Matching Puzzle Game, where three or four letters with pictures made a word. After watching his older sisters' breeze through it, he said, "Mommy, that's too hard for me." I told him, "Let's try together, I will play with you" (note, I didn't say help).

I didn't expect him to match all the words or even search through all the pieces, to find three or four out of a hundred, to put together. It would have overwhelmed him. I started by putting three pieces that matched, mixed up in front of him, not making it obvious. It took him a while to fit the three together, but halfway through, he gained confidence and practice.

By the end, about forty-five minutes later, I stopped putting three in front of him. He figured out there were concepts, images, and parts he recognized, out of the whole, and he didn't need any more help. He was so proud when he finished. The next time I brought out a similar type of toy he knew what to do.

Any manipulative I used I would also set up, for at least a jump start, to the activity. I would hide small plastic balls under stacking cups or stack the cups on top of each other. I would stack the ABC blocks into a tower or spell the child's name or make simple words out of the letters. I would have balls ready to go next to a slide tower, put a few pegs in the peg board, or begin a base to a block structure. **A child cannot resist the desire to explore something in front of them or take over.**

I also would add and rotate in wooden food sets, food cutting board set, cake or pizza sets, to integrate with the House Area of learning. Sometimes I would bring in things from my own kitchen, like pots or pans, measuring cups or measuring spoons, or a rolling pin. Other items were plastic tea sets I would set up with the cups on the saucers and the little spoons in the cups. I also rotated in medical supplies or baby supplies and accessories. There are so many options.

PLAYHOUSES, GARAGES, DOLLHOUSES: For playhouses, garages, and dollhouses, until around four-years-old, I would set up and stage them. If I put out a barn or farmhouse, I would set up a few fences and take out our collection of farm animals or horses, and put them in the right plac-

es (the farmer in the tractor, the horse in the stable, and so on). As they got older, and sometimes just to change things up, I would offer a bin of farm animals next to the barn, but not set it up. This added to the experience, especially when the play became more involved. Doing this created more "work" and encouraged self motivation.

If I put the dinosaur collection out, I would put out the mat below, set up the trees, and group the dinosaurs together, putting the larger of the same with the smaller of the same. I put the "mommy dinosaur and baby dinosaur" together. I would also put the water animals in the pretend water and put some drinking by the stream. The children began to recognize water animals from land animals, and so on.

GETTING STARTED

1. Table (train table or table with a lip)

2. Manipulatives (four to five options)
   Years 0-2+: set of large Lego blocks, sorting cube, stacking cups or rings
   Years 3-6+: magnetic shapes, tower building sets, connecting sets

3. Puzzles (four to five options)
   Years 0-2+: wooden five to seven-piece sets
   Years 3-6+: ten to twenty-piece sets, floor puzzles

4. Playhouse & Figurines (one to two options)
   Years 0-2+: farmhouse with a set of animals
   Years 3-6+: dollhouse with five or more figurines, parking garage with five or more vehicles, dinosaur forest with a mat and five or more dinosaurs

5. Other (one to three options)
   Years 0-2+: food cutting kits, wooden magnetic boy or girl dress-up set, lacing cards

Years 3-6+: spell and learn, puzzle, picture boards (see and spell, self correcting, sequencing sets

Materials for the Center Activity Table

For the Centery Activity Table get various age appropriate puzzles, blocks, playhouses, garages, figurines, and more. The options are limitless. **Refer to Part I-II: Types of Toys & Equipment, Open- Ended Toy Suggestions & Structured Toys Suggestions and Part II: Construction & Block Area, Materials for the Construction & Block Area.**

How to Set Up, Facilitate, & Use the Center Activity Table

1. Offer and rotate a variety of open-ended and structured-toys daily

2. Talk about the objects; names, patterns, colors, shapes, numbers, sizes, other ("This is a horse", "This is a triangle")

3. Show different options; stacking or aligning shapes in different ways (the farmer feeds the horse hay, the triangle can't stand on its tip)

4. Set up each figurine in its right place (the pilot in the cockpit, the school bus driver in the bus)

5. Suggest what an object is used for, show how it moves, what it does (a horse gallops and neighs, a triangle could be a roof)

6. Play with them, be a character, or assist with an activity

7. Help when a child is having trouble after trying many times, show them how to do it

8. Comment on a pattern or compliment successful completion of a task ("You finished and didn't give up!", after successfully putting together a puzzle independently)

9. Be curious about their discoveries; ask what they figured out, learned, remembered, other ("What shape is that?" "How did you know how to make that structure?")

10. Suggest props or other toys that could be used during play (place a figurine to drive the car)

House Area

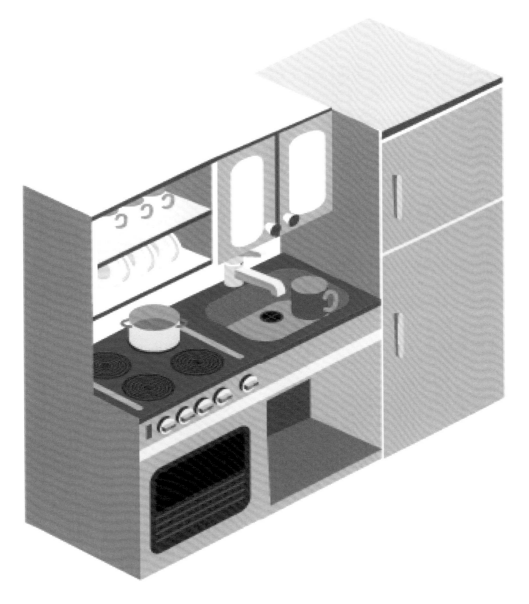

The House Area is a small scale re-creation of home. In this learning area a child takes on the roles of family members, relatives, friends, teachers, doctors, and others they meet, or are exposed to in their lives.

The House Area is where you will see and hear children work out roles and responsibilities, relationships, act out what they have seen or heard,  and invent their own play scenarios. They will model their play after you and other people in their lives.

Using the play phones, for example, you may hear them having a conversation with grandmother or "the boss"; while cooking on the stove, vacuuming, working on the computer, or washing dishes. This area is a place to safely practice and copy what they see. Taking on an adult role gives children a sense of control and power, a space to do bigger things, and develop an understanding of how the world works.

You will also hear language emerging, and **the more words supplied by the adults in their lives, the more expanded their vocabulary.** For example, if a child is playing doctor with a medical kit, explain what a stethoscope is and why a doctor uses it (you may need to redirect them and show him or her where the heart is).

When a child is exposed to a new situation like a wedding or visits a sick relative in a hospital, you will see them act this out in pretend play. They may pretend to be a bride, doctor, or a patient. If there is no other child, they will often use a baby doll or a stuffed animal to play a different role. This is also a great opportunity to join in and offer to play a role, not only to participate, but to engage in discussion and offer insight. You can explain what marriage is or what an IV or oxygen mask is and used for. You can see how teaching

and learning can happen in all these moments!

Children also learn lot from each other, whether from older siblings, relatives, or friends on play dates. Children will assign roles and tasks and even words to their friends. They may say, for example, "You be the dog, and go lie down," or "No, don't say that, you say 'Yes, honey,' and then take out the garbage." You will also hear some language that will need redirection, such as "He seed the dog," to which you will respond, "Oh, he saw the dog?" By responding to a child's speech in this way, he or she will get the message without the distraction or embarrassment of having made a mistake.

The House Area does not require much set up but is usually one of the most used areas. Creating new settings for dramatic play promotes learning, not only in acting things out but learning the content as they do. Older children (four and above) love to model and pretend play.

Some days I would take the baby dolls out of their storage area and set them up in the

highchair or stroller, dressed, with their bottles and other accessories ready to go. Other times, I would take out the cash register and toy money, which would trigger a game of buying and selling. When I took out the medical kit and medical supplies, this would trigger playing doctor, nurse, dentist, or other medically themed play.

The more resources provided and rotated in this space (such as various costumes or supplies), the more children will role play and engage in dramatic play (restaurant, gym, library, store, and more). Simple things often work best., such as old credit cards or stamps. By introducing new materials and props you can facilitate an entirely new experience each time. You can leave themes set up for weeks. Themes are also wonderful for play dates.

Have the children help set up and think of ideas to encourage creativity. Setting it up is just as much fun. Use your imagination. This is a space rich in play experience.

Learning Connections Tied to the House Area

- **Practice caring for and nurturing dolls, stuffed animals, or each other** *(Physical, Social & Emotional)*

- **Model, re-enact, and act out interactions with family members or friends** *(Language, Social & Emotional, Cognitive)*

- **Pretend to clean, cook, vacuum** *(Cognitive, Physical)*

- **Play dress up and pretend to be other things like animals, a nurse, a chef** *(Language, Cognitive, Physical, Social & Emotional)*

- **Facilitate a theme, set up, collect, and organize items** *(Language, Cognitive, Physical, Social & Emotional)*

GETTING STARTED

1. Kitchen

2. Food & Utensils
(four to five options)
   Years 0-2+: One
   set of food, dishes,
   and utensils
   Years 3-6+: Two to
three different play sets (BBQ, pizza cutting, sushi)

3. Dress-up clothes
   Years 0-2+: One to two hats, pull-on skirts, jacket, gloves
   Years 3-6+: Two to four costumes, old button-up shirts,
   pants, accessories

4. Babies & Items for Babies (one to two options)
   Years 0-2+: One to two life-size baby dolls, highchair, cri
   Years 3-6+: Clothes for babies, stroller, feeding kits

5. Table & Chairs

6. Unbreakable mirror

7. Other (one to two options)
   Years 0-2+: Child-size vacuum, broom, shopping cart (great
   for encouraging walking)
   Years 3-6+: Cash register, fake money

Kitchen

A kitchen will be one of the most used pieces of equipment in a play-room. It is a worthwhile investment (especially if you have more than one

child)! Be sure the kitchen has a sink, oven, refrigerator, and cooktop stove. I felt a kitchen constructed of wood for inside was best. They last the longest and are very sturdy. The texture of wood is natural and soft for a child. The indoor kitchen I purchased was a Melissa & Doug Classic Delux, which retailed for $279.

I also picked up many different types of plastic kitchens, that I found free on the side of the road. I used these as options to rotate into the playroom (to make things fresh), put them down in the basement during snowed-in days, or to use outside.

Plastic kitchens are wonderful during warmer months, for outside water and sand play (because they can get wet and clean easily)! I would set up the kitchen next to our Sensory Table **(Refer to Part II: Sensory Table)** filled with sand, a few buckets of water or a hose, and it became a whole new integrated learning activity. "Cooking" with sand and water is super fun.

I have been served mud pies, pizza, soup, cake, and so on! It does get super messy so if you do incorporate water or sand, make sure you set this up in a space you don't care will get wet and dirty, and is easy to clean!

There are basic items you always want to keep in

the kitchen. Imagine you are trying to outfit a brand-new kitchen. What basics would you need; pots, pans, teapot, utensils, bowls, cups, plates, coffee maker, and more! Great items to rotate in this area from the Center Activity Table toys are Melissa and Doug food sets (like a food cutting set, pizza set, birthday cake and candle set, BBQ set, sushi set, or other). It is important to have a variety of textures for sensory development.

Collecting used items from families with older children getting rid of things, at yard sales, or social media marketplaces are a great option. Most toys are super easy to clean with bleach!

Dress-Up Clothes

Dressing up is one of a child's favorite thing to do. Imagine a Halloween party year round! I added to this collection over time; old shirts, skirts, pants, dresses, hats, scarves, jewelry, shoes, purses, suitcase, briefcase, plastic eye frames, sunglasses, and more. As things were outgrown, new items were swapped in. There should be a mix of dress-up clothes for both boys and girls, and gender neutral clothes (even if you just have one gender).

I collected lots of hand-me downs, including dress-up clothes from grandparents, cousins, and friends. Grandparents often have

lots of old items like bags, jewelry, old watches, shoes, necklaces, glasses, and more (*and they love to give these to their grandchildren*).

Old Halloween costumes also work great, both adult and children's costumes. Each year a new costume went into the play pile. One year my daughter was a rabbit and my son was a dog, and these costumes were used often. Once these costumers became too small, I simply cut the feet off until they no longer fit some years later. I did buy a few important outfits to add to the diversity and to enhance pretend and imaginative play. I bought a nurse and doctor smock, a fireman coat, hat, badge, and extinguisher, and a police jacket, hat, badge, and handcuffs. These roles are a big part of childhood. Children see these daily service heroes on TV, in parades, while in the car (when they hear a siren), and are taught about these roles in school.

My middle daughter wanted a cowgirl outfit for her birthday one year. It came with a gun and holster. This began gunplay in our home. There are differences in opinion, but research has found that boys who play cops and robbers, military games, or with guns are no more aggressive than those who do not. Surprisingly, studies show no link between playing with toy weapons in childhood and aggression in adulthood.

They can't tell if it's wired into the brain or through social learning, but the differences between how boys and girl's role play is strong. At six, my son often played the role of the hero when my girls were playing princesses or movie stars. His role was often the police officer to protect them, or he rescued them from danger. However, he equally liked being the monster or villain! Allow and encourage girls and boys to experience and pretend to be different roles, especially different roles typically female or male

To store the clothes and make them easy to access for play, I purchased one large clear, three-drawer, freestanding stackable storage bin. The clothes were not organized, just thrown in. I left big items like the fireman extinguisher and hats on top. I added a few hooks to hang are few of the jackets near the play kitchen. Hooks serve a multi-purpose to teach cleanup and how to hang items up and pull them down. Each thing in the playroom is designed to teach and help a child develop important skills.

Despite gender tendencies, all children love to dress up as different things. Dressing up is also always one of the favorite things to do when friends come over. This picture was from a Saturday night sleepover, unstaged!

Babies & Items for Babies

Every child should have life-sized baby dolls to play with. Babies are natural and all children identify with them. Baby dolls make children feel

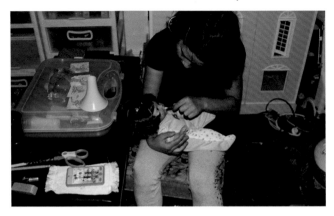

big and grown up. They will model and role play how they are and have been cared for. Playing with a baby doll touches all areas of learning.

A child will act as if a baby doll is a real person and interact with them this way. They will perform actions in sequence such as feeding, bathing, and putting the doll to bed. Playing with a baby doll gives them the opportunity to practice appropriately holding and using items (such as spoons, bottles, cups, forks, bowls, and so on).

Boys love babies too! When my son was three, he adored motorcycles, loud noises, rough play, trucks and cars, but also loved babies as much as my daughters did. We often forget, with the constant gender conditioning in the media, that toys are really gender neutral to a child.

Items for the dolls should include clothing, diapers, bottles, onesies, binkies, blankets, bottles, stroller, miniature play pen, highchair, carrier, car seat, and other. If you have had a baby recently, you may still have some of these items. Baby toys are also a fun option.

Real-life size items are often better than toy versions, especially clothing (hats, shoes, bottles, binkies, diapers, other). But some toys will work better in a smaller size. It is easier for a child to maneuver a toy sized crib or stroller, for example, instead of a full sized one. They will able to pick it up and take it around the house more easily.

Children will practice dressing and undressing the toy babies; putting a hat on their head, zipping up clothing, putting socks or shoes on, pulling up diapers or pants, putting on onesies, a shirt, buttoning buttons and snaps, and more. Taking clothing off is usually mastered before putting them on. Kids often find it easier to practice these skills on something or someone else before they can do it themselves. However, note that most children just leave babies and dolls naked after they are done playing with them.

Conversing during play and stating the names of items is an important part of facilitation. It not only increases vocabulary and comprehension, but also enhances social and emotional development. For example, you can ask your child questions while they play, "Is the baby sleeping?" or "Why is the baby crying? Is she hungry?"

Dolls are also great for teaching body parts. For example, "Where is the baby's toe?" or "Where are the baby's eyes?" It helps very young children understand eyes are not only on their doll's face, but on all faces, including their own.

Diversity can enhance the experience too (having a variety of dolls, Caucasian, African American, Asian, Hispanic, or other)! Some children will prefer to play these scenarios with stuffed animals, miniatures of people, Barbie dolls or other dolls, rather than real-life baby dolls.

If you have younger children or are expecting a baby, baby dolls are a wonderful tool to introduce and transition an older child for the event. You can use this opportunity to expose the child to what will happen and give them a chance to experience things in a safe environment and place. You can teach the child how to gently hold, touch, burp, change the baby, and more. The more items you have for a coming baby, the more items you can introduce into the playroom at different times.

Table & Chairs

A child sized table and chairs will be used frequently! Children will use it when serving pretend food, eating a snack, setting up a restaurant, crafting, games, and more. I began with a small Fisher Price plastic table with four chairs (that I picked up on the side of the road). *I always grabbed any large plastic structures or toys, because they are great to rotate in, and free! Plastics are easy to clean with a power washer or bleach!* Children quickly outgrow baby and toddler equipment. I do not recommend buying baby or toddler chairs and table, unless you do not mind replacing them after a year or two. I also found I

was frequently a participant sitting in one of the chairs. Just make sure whatever table and chairs you use are solid and sturdy and will not tip or flip backward especially with babies and toddlers.

When my children became more mobile and transitioned to a separate Writing Area **(refer to Part II: Writing Area)**, I rotated the small plastic table and chairs in and out of the playroom to add variety to pretend play. I also rotated the equipment outdoors in warmer months the basement during colder months. A child sized table and chairs is a heavily used piece of equipment.

Unbreakable Mirror

This may seem like an odd item to list, but mirrors are wonderful in establishing identity and self-recognition. Young children can also develop pre-reading skills from watching themselves talk in a mirror (practicing pronunciation and vocabulary). Children at any age love to look and watch themselves in a mirro!

Unbreakable mirrors are bendable and made from plastic materials. Twelve inches by forty-eight inches is a great full-length size for a child.

I did not mount our mirror on a wall. I left it near the kitchen and dress-up clothes (so it was moveable). Things move a lot in a playroom). My children loved being able to move it and put it on the ground. When they were very small, they would lie on it, make funny faces, and kiss themselves.

Mirrors encourage self-awareness and self-care (recognizing teeth, the difference between messy hair and brushed hair, when faces are dirty and need to be washed, clothes are backwards, and more). Small hand mirros are also a great addition.

When children are older, they will use mirrors to watch themselves play, have puppet shows, pretend stuffed animals or baby dolls are talking, and more. The use of mirrors eventually progresses to seeing how they look, playing dress up, dancing, putting on makeup, or modeling.

Materials for the House Area

1. **Kitchen**
2. **Dress-up clothes** (costumes, adult hand-me-downs, hats, gloves, jewelry, accessories, other)
3. **Life-size baby dolls & items for babies** (stroller, changing station, crib, highchair, diapers, clothing, other)
4. **Small table & chairs**
5. **Unbreakable mirror**
6. **Various fake plastic and wooden food items**

7. **Dishes, cups, pots, pans**
8. **Kitchen utensils & Tupperware**
9. **Cleaning items** (mop, broom, vacuum, other)
10. **Iron & ironing board**
11. **Pocket books, bags, briefcases, wallets**

12. **Soft space & sitting items** (small cushions, bean bag chair, ottoman, other)
13. **Telephones** (toy phone or old cell phones)
14. **Pencils and pads, calculator**
15. **Calendar, camera, photos, rugs**
16. **Decorations** (pictures, non-toxic or plastic plants)
17. **Materials used in a house** (baking pans, oven mitts, coffee maker, blender, table cloth, curtains, other)
18. **Camping supplies & equipment** (tent, canteens, BBQ kits, grill, sleeping bags, pretend food, other)
19. **Other**

Many of these supplies can be found inexpensively, in your cupboards, basement, at yard sales, flea markets, thrift shops, garage sales, from grand-

parents or relatives, or large retail or discount stores. Many I just rotated in from our life-size kitchen and allowed my children to take things to play with if they chose (measuring cups, non-sharp utensils, old prescription bottles with caps, and more).

How to Set Up, Facilitate, & Use the House Area

1. Set up different types of pretend play (grocery store, clothing store, veterinarian, school, hospital, other)

2. Talk about the objects; names, patterns, colors, shapes, numbers, sizes, other and roles ("This is a spoon," or "A veterinarian cares for animals")

3. Label items and objects (sink, oven, apple)

4. Show how to use the materials (the pot goes on the burner, the milk in the refrigerator, demonstrate how to organize money in a cash register)

5. Facilitate role play (discuss what a person's job is or why they do what they do; a doctor uses a stethoscope to listen to your heart, a cashier exchanges money)

6. Play with them (be a character or help with an activity, for example, be the patient, or shopper, or student in class)

7. Help when a child is having trouble (after many tries, show them how to do it, for example, put the onesies on the baby for them, or open the cash register)

8. Comment on the way they are playing ("You are a good mother feeding the baby its bottle," or "You are very gentle with your bear when you dress her.")

9. Ask who they are, what they are doing, and why ("What are you cooking on the stove?" or "Does your baby have a fever?")

10. Suggest props or other toys that could be used during play (ask your child to make eggs in the frying pan, or deliver a letter to the stuffed Giraffe when playing post office)

Additional Options

Playing Store

All children have the experience of going to many different types of stores! Setting up a store offers so many opportunities for learning. I usually facilitate the first few minutes (help set up, play as a shopper or cashier), but if your children have ever gone shopping with you, they know what to do; exchange money, count, plan, organize, stock, bag, shop, and more.

I had my children collect empty recycled boxes or plastics; cereal boxes, maple syrup, cracker boxes, pasta boxes, egg cartons, juice or milk containers, and more. Whatever they can find that is clean from the recycle bins or cupboards, to set up and sell, is great for playing store.

It is fun for all ages to make; fake money, signs, price tags, labels, credit cards (old library cards or business cards work great), and more.

If you don't have a cash register, a calculator will work too. If you don't have a shopping cart an old Easter basket or any small basket of will suffice. Add a few used plastic bags for filling and bagging groceries after someone has paid.

MATERIALS: cash register, homemade or plastic money, coupons, supermarket ads, bags, stickers for tags and prices, old credit cards, shopping baskets or carts, signs for different store sections (dairy, produce, other), **canned goods, empty containers, smocks, hangers, clothes, or other**

Playing Post Office & Deliveries

This is so much fun to play. It helps develop the abilities of writing, correspondence, and addressing!

A visit to the post office can lead to a study of how mail gets from one

place to another, and the different jobs people hold. This is a great activity to teach a child's address and the concept of being on a street, in a town, in a state, in a country. Explaining an address can lead to a study of routes, roads, and maps.

Mail a real letter to a grandparent or friend! The entire process is fun; writing a letter, stuffing an envelope, addressing and stamping it, to dropping it in a mailbox at the post office. There are great sites for older children with pen pals around the world, too.

Deliveries from companies like Federal Express and UPS are so common today, that facilitating this theme is another great alternative. Set up a pretend warehouse with old recyclable boxes or role play a delivery person.

MATERIALS: telephone books, envelopes, pens, zip code directories, junk mail, magazines, old letters, old stamps, ink pads and stampers, stickers, scales to weigh (kitchen scales work great)**, boxes** (for a warehouse, to mail a package, or to make a pretend mailbox)**, signs, or other**

Playing Office

Most children have experienced an office setting, like a principal's office or a doctor's office, and many have a parent who works in one. Children love to pretend to be the boss. Providing an old laptop or smart phone works great. You will hear them having conversations, giving orders, taking calls, pretend typing and more (acting just like you). One of my funniest videos is my son imitating me on the phone at four years old, "Busy, busy, busy. It is such a busy day. I have so much to do."

MATERIALS: pads of paper, old or laptop, old smartphone, calculators, business cards, calendars, briefcases, stapler, folders, paper clips, post-it notes, scissors, hole-punchers, notepads, rulers, pens, pencils, or other

Climbing & Movement

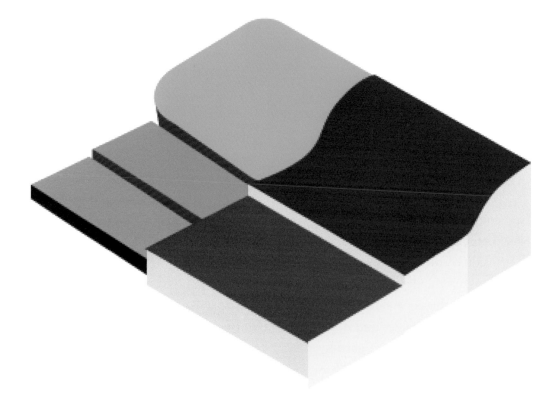

The Climbing & Movement Area should be a dedicated space for movement. This does not require a lot of space for small children, if the equipment is child-sized and rotated into a playroom. The activities will evolve

as a child grows from basic dancing and hopping, to Sit & Spins, to jumping and running.

This area is less about the type of equipment, as it is in remembering a child needs to move his or her body constantly, and should be encouraged to do so throughout the day. Playing music from the Music Area is often enough stimulate dancing and movement. Very young children (zero to two years) will use their bodies just accessing and exploring the toys you set up in the playroom. Ages two and older will need more facilitation and types of equipment, for example, an indoor slide or hop balls.

Encourage anything that gets them moving and using their bodies. This could include dancing, jumping jacks, hopping on one foot, crawling around pretending to be an animal, or even yoga with you. It's as if energy builds up inside of them and must get out. Allocating time for movement also helps break up the day and playtime.

I purchased a floor climbing structure that could be taken apart and changed. As babies and toddlers, my children could practice climbing and slide down without getting hurt. It was also a place for the children to lay on or bring toys like cars to slide down. As they got older, they would use it to make a fort to hide in, to play separately from the others, to read on, to create

some elaborate play scenario, or simply relax.

By the time they transitioned from walking to running, their physical needs were greater, and we had to go outside more often. **Refer to Part II: Outdoor Area**.

During the winter or on cold and rainy days, my entire unfinished basement was set up for the children to use. I converted it into open space and child proofed it as much as I could. I created a track on the concrete floor using duct tape, to establish a path, to ride their sit-on scooters, tricycles, roller blades, bicycles, to play tag, or just run around. In the basement, they can jump, run, dance, throw things, and make a mess. I also purchased an indoor inflatable bounce house that fit four small children. My children loved this when they were small (around two, which lasted until my oldest was seven).

As children get older, needing movement transitions to requiring daily exercise, I found if they do not get at least one hour of movement, running around inside or outside, they pick on each other or fight. I even set up my elliptical trainer and stationary bicycle in my living room. The kids use them more than I do (apparently these are fun, and their friends use them just as much). I also have an exercise ball and two rollers they use constantly. Whatever works! Children need to move and release energy, especially school-aged children who must sit quietly most of the day. **Movement is a critical part of every child's day.**

GETTING STARTED

1. Climbing Structure

2. Gross Motor Equipment (one to five options)

Years 0-2+ years: rocking horse, obstacle courses, balance beam

Years 3-6+ years: indoor slide, riding scooter, Sit & Spin

Materials for the Climbing & Movement Area

1. **Climbing structure or tumbling mat**
2. **Sit & Spins**
3. **Hop Balls**
4. **Doorway Gym**
5. **Indoor plastic slide**
6. **Rocking horse**
7. **Dance barre**
8. **Parachute**
9. **Sit-On scooters, ride on Toy, tricycle,**
10. **Wagon or Pull Cart**
11. **Jump ropes, Hula Hoops**
12. **Fold up mazes**
13. **Roller skates**
14. **Balance beam & bars, Balance Board**
15. **Indoor swing or Yoga swing**
16. **Pogo Jumper**
17. **Mini trampoline** (with bar for toddlers)
18. **Stepping & Balance Stones**
19. **Indoor dome climber**

Most of these items I acquired from the side of the road or yard sales. I would typically only bring in one or two items at a time and change this equipment every few days or weekly, rather than daily. I would also encourage use of items from the House Area, such as the shopping cart and baby stroller to promote movement (take the baby for a walk).

How to Set Up, Facilitate, & Use the Climbing & Movement Area

1. Rotate different obstacles and goals for movement (for example, musical instruments, scarves or streamers to dance with)

2. Explain physical health and body parts and what their function are (when you exercise your heart is beating fast to push blood through your body to bring your muscles more oxygen)

3. Demonstrate using different body parts (hopping on one foot) **and assist through different activities** (hold one hand to help)

4. Encourage movement often (walk the baby, turn on music and dance), **refer to Part II: Listening Area**

5. Exercise with them (stretch, do yoga, jump rope, play hopscotch, and more)

6. Help when a child is having trouble (after trying many times show him or her how to do it)

7. Commend them on a successful completion of a task ("You did it! You pumped on the swing without needing a push!")

Playhouse Area

Playhouses are structures that children can climb in and out of, and imagine and pretend they are big in their own little world. Children love to hide, snuggle up, and play in small spaces. This area is very easy to manage. I had a few different fold-up houses to rotate in and out of the playroom, and one we made from an extra large appliance box. The fold-up houses were made of a tent like material with an entrance. Small regular camping tents also work.

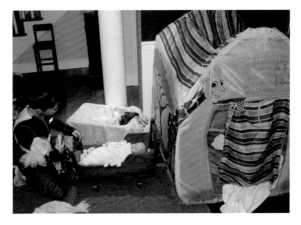

Children will pretend playhouses are a post office, ice cream truck, airplane, veterinarian clinic, an island safe from sharks, a hiding place, a hotel, and more. You will see them bring stuffed animals, cushions, blankets and pillows, read books inside, and pretend play with different toys and friends. If something is missing, this is usually where you will find it! I never knew what scenario I was going to walk into. These houses are a simple addition, but a very powerful resource and play space.

Home Depot or any hardware store is happy to recycle boxes and give them away. By using a new stove box, I made a roof (with the top flaps), covered it with a cellophane sheet, and cut in a door and windows on each side. I then had my children decorate it with markers, stickers, and tape. Because the cardboard was so sturdy, it lasted almost four years of aggressive use Yes! Four! I rotated it in and out of different areas in the house including the basement.

All different sized boxes are a super fun alternative to rotate in this space (or into the Climbing & Movement area). Empty boxes serve as a place to hide, a house, a plane, a boat, a car, components of a train, and more.

GETTING STARTED

1. A playhouse, large appliance box, or camping tent
2. Cushions, small blankets

Materials for the Playhouse Area

1. **Various playhouses, tents, or extra large appliance box**
2. **Different sized empty boxes** (small to large)
3. **Cushions, blankets, pillows, other**
4. **Resources from the House Area or Center Activity Table**

How to Set Up, Facilitate, & Use the Playhouse Area

To facilitate this area simply take out a different playhouse every week or every other week, depending on how much it is used. Sometimes take one out of the playroom altogether and leave the space empty, if you feel they had exhausted their interest in using one. After a few weeks transition it back in, and voila, it will be used like new again!

Scenario suggestions I offered were similar to the suggestions in the House Area (for example, a place we would visit like the chiropractor, an urgent care facility, or Starbucks). Indoor camping is a super fun activity. Once an idea is ignited the entire area will come to life. Toys from the life-size kitchen, Center Activity Table and House Area will be brought in, such as BBQ kits and dress up clothes.

Art Area

The Art Area is where a childs p'ainting, pasting, coloring, drawing, writing, crafts, and design will occur. Art is putting the hands, eyes, and ears to work through trial and error. For young children, producing art is very basic. Art activities involve all the senses and help wire the brain for successful learning.

Art is expressive. It helps to develop essential thinking such as memory, interpretation, and representation of what is imagined or seen. It involves careful observation of things in the world and transforming it into a form.

Fine motor skills will develop and mature over time, with increased mastery over the tools provided. Over time you will see unrecognizable images evolve into houses, animals, different landscapes, to detailed faces. Art has many forms, and all art is unique and beautiful.

Art activities do not have to be elaborate or complicated. Simply changing the materials and resources are a child needs. Supplying a variety of crayons, colored pencils, markers, chalk, paints, watercolors, glue, glitter, or other, along with different types of paper or paintable materials, triggers the necessary creativity.

At first, I had a simple easel set up in the playroom (I often moved if to the kitchen or our mudroom), usually with one or two colors of paint, a few brushes, and a large pad of paper. I also had smocks to wear while painting. Art is messy and there is no way around it.

Wood, cardboard boxes, coffee filters, even pinecones and rocks can all be used as art tools. I have a garden full of painted rocks. As the children got older and worked on more complex projects like painting small objects or making models or kits, I transitioned them to a separate dedicated area in my kitchen, which became the Art and Writing Area of Learning. **Refer to PART II: Writing Area.**

Types of Artwork

• **Draw on** (different types of paper, materials, objects, boards, other)

• **Draw with** (markers, chalk, crayons, pencils, bingo daubers, water, other)

• **Paint on** (easel, washable walls or surfaces, erasable boards, paper, objects, rocks, blacktop, cardboard, other)

• **Paint with** (paint, water, watercolors, fingers, brushes, popsicle sticks, Q-tips, straws, leaves, toothpicks, other)

• **Cut with** (scissors, saws carving tools, plastic knives, clippers, dental floss, string, cutters, other)

• **Construct** (paper, wood, Popsicle sticks, Q-tips, Papier Mache, wire, string, tape, foil, other)

• **Connect things** (glue, tape, wire, nails, sticks, elastic bands, tape, stickers, staples, paper clips, string, yarn, other)

• **Mold** (floam, slime, moon sand, Oobleck, playdough, clay, plaster, putty, other)

• **Clean up** (sponges, brushes, rags, paper towels, brooms, dust pans, soap, mops, tooth-brushes, bottle cleaners, other)

A lot of materials do not need to be purchased or available all at once. My collection evolved with age. Younger children only need a few supplies at a time. Toddlers, for example, do not need more than an easel, a couple paint brushes, a few primary paint colors, some paper, a few large markers, some chalk, or large crayons.

One art activity a day is enough for a small child (until around the age of two, and it will depend on your child's interests and abilities).

One day I would set up a painting activity, the next day a coloring activity with crayons, and the next moon sand with playdough accessories.

Older children will spend more time drawing, writing, and crafting. Once they are school aged, they can access materials themselves and use as they feel. Although, even older children still benefit from facilitation (for example, suggesting making Christmas ornaments as gifts).

Rotating materials such as Playdough, floam, moon sand, and putty into the Art Area or as a manipulative on the Center Activity Table, are great for any age, and should be woven into a regular routine. **Manipulating materials into form and making objects target the same fundamentals.** *Homemade playdough is easy to make and a great resource to always have available.* **Refer to Part III: Homemade Playdough Recipe.**

Coloring books and miscellaneous paper products were always accessible in a bottom drawer in my kitchen. Art and crafting has become an integral part of our home.

GETTING STARTED

1. Easel

2. Materials (4 to 5 options)

Years 0-2+:

- 1 large pad of paper
- 3 to 5 large brushes
- 5 basic washable paint colors
- Paint cups
- Box of five large crayons or markers
- Scrap paper or small pad of paper
- Smock

Years 3-6+:

- 3 to 5 different sizes and types of paper
- 5 to 10 different-size brushes
- 2 to 3 different themes of coloring books
- Box of 12 to 24 crayons
- 1 set of watercolors
- 1 pair of child-size scissors
- 1 roll of masking tape or scotch tape

Materials for the Art Area

- **Easel** (single or double sided or tabletop)
- **Paper** (different sizes and types: large sheets of white paper, pads of paper, lined, unlined, construction paper, other)
- **Paints** (washable, finger paints, watercolors, acrylics, bubble/fabric paint, other)
- **Various sizes of paint brushes**
- **Boxes of crayons** (large size for smaller children)

- **Bingo daubers** (non-toxic)
- **Colored pencils**
- **Coffee filters**
- **Chalk board**
- **Chalk & chalk tools** (white and colored, thick and thin)
- **Various types of markers** (large size for smaller children)
- **Plastic eye droppers**
- **Scissors** (age appropriate)
- **Paste and glue** (glue sticks or glue with brushes)
- **Collage & miscellaneous materials** (old magazines, paper scraps, brochures, ribbons, other)
- **Magnet board & alphabet magnets**
- **Dry erase board & erasable markers**
- **Playdough, shaving cream, Floam, Oobleck, moon sand, putty, other & accessories** (plastic knives, rolling pin, plastic dishes, cutting tools, clay hammers, cookie cutters, other)

All different types of materials and recyclables can be used for crafts. I would often take cardboard from the recycling bin and lay it on the ground outside. I would let them paint with fingers, brushes, Q-tips, leaves, or even pinecones.

Painting different objects and textures with water is a wonderful sensory activity and clean up is easy. You will be amazed at how much fun they have. Give a child some old paint brushes, a bucket of water or cups, and let them paint any surface (the house, the sidewalk, the driveway, walls in the basement, even themselves). Mixing chalk and water also makes for a great and easy activity (especially if you run out of paint).

Try different textures and sizes of materials and resources (for example, use tissue paper, toilet paper, or napkins and watching the materials dissolve). **Art often becomes a science experiment.**

Once these resources are established as tools for children, it will amaze you what they do with them. Just offer them and let them play.

How to Set Up, Facilitate, & Use the Art Area

1. Set up various activities and crafts daily that are child safe and developmentally appropriate

2. Offer different sizes and types of materials and resources on a regular basis

3. Encourage children to experiment and get messy, turn Art activities into science experiments

4. Demonstrate the right use of materials (hold a paint brush or pencil the right way)

5. Provide activities to complete, or a sample of a craft

(fold the edges of a piece of paper and make a paper fan, or draw a letter or shape with dots to practice cutting)

6. Commend and display their artwork

7. Join them in coloring, painting, or crafting

Reading Area

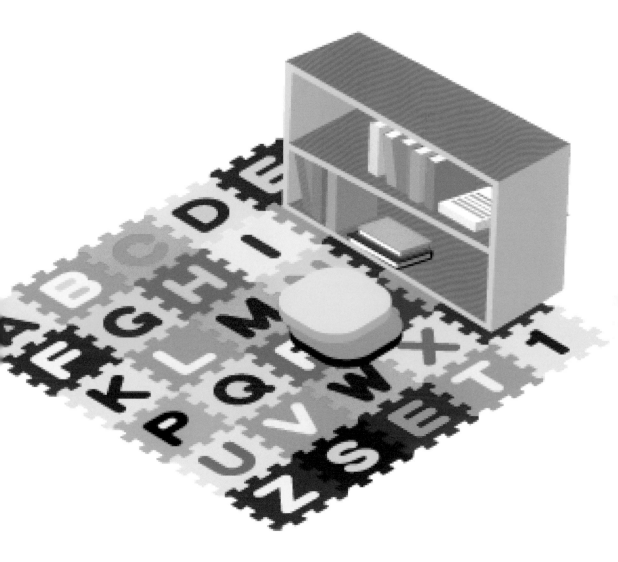

This learning area is a space dedicated to reading. Establishing a place specifically for books creates a sense of importance, and it will naturally become part of a child's environment and routine. Have a sitting area (with cushions, mats, soft chair, or spot for relaxation), a bookcase or bin, and a variety of books.

A child does not have to have fluency in reading to appreciate, or benefit from books! Books are full of magic and mystery, rich images and colors, without even knowing how to read the words. Reading isn't the only purpose of a story, or the story itself. Each story contains an adventure, full of beautiful scenes and details, characters and messages. (Audio books are also important and part of the Reading Area but covered in the Listening Area). **Refer to Part II: Listening Area.**

Even before a child can read, exposure to many different types of books is important, fiction and non-fiction. Children's brain activity and imaginations soar as they look at the brilliant colors, photographs, and artistic creations on each page. The thought put into a picture book is incredible. Informational books are equally as important to teach words and concepts at early age and information as they get older.

My children often created and made up their own stories when they were not yet able to read. This is the beginnings of literacy development. A a child begins to recognize some words and starts to fill in the blanks, and context of unknown words. This is the basis of comprehension.

Books should be age appropriate, easily accessible, and rotated frequently. I used to do it weekly, sometimes more often if they spent a lot of time in that space and had looked at each book more than a few times. I also had a large bin of books in each of my children's rooms to read a book before a nap and bedtime.

When they were young, I would put out two or three age appropriate books every morning on the floor or on top of the climbing structure for

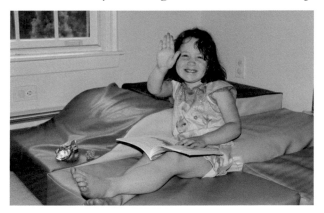

them to find (a mix of word books and picture books). It was a welcome surprise. Each one of my children flipped through the pages and immersed themselves in images for long periods of time, years before they could read.

I never pressed or focused on words until it became developmentally important (and you will know because they will start recognizing and calling out letters and eventually words). At first, I bought a ton of books but realized this was a major expense. Instead, I started a collection by going to yard sales, and ultimately created a routine of taking the children to the local library once a week. The maximum check out is fifty books at our library, and we pretty much maxed out that limit each time (audio books included, especially for children with learning delays or disabilities).

My children used to get just as excited going to the library as the toy store! Even though only one of them, early on, could read, the others spent hours finding books, looking at pictures, and flipping pages. Most libraries also have weekly activities and a small play area, which is a great break if you are looking for something productive for them to do.

A felt board and felt board stories are another great option to tell stories and can provide hours of learning as imaginations soar. These also are easy to make out of felt rather than buy. You can replicate the classics, like Little Red Riding Hood, The Three Little Pigs, or can make up your own stories. Children will also use these pieces to pretend play with or tell their own stories.

Reading has always been a primary routine in each of my children's days, and it is one of the greatest investments we can give our children. A love of reading stays with a child forever, helps with literacy and the transition to formal school. Reading is not only a privilege, but a gift.

GETTING STARTED

1. **Bookcase or book bin**
2. **Cushions** (two to three)
3. **Various books** (a library is the most affordable way to
   rotate books)

How to Set Up, Facilitate, & Use the Reading Area

1. Provide interesting and colorful books that are age appropriate

2. Take your children to the library

3. Encourage your children to find books they like

4. Read a book (at least twice a day)

5. Talk to your children about the story (pictures, the characters, ask what they think about them, and what might happen next)

6. Use the images to teach new words (increase vocabulary)

7. Provide books on subjects or topics that interest them (for example, if a boy likes monster trucks provide books about truck or construction vehicles)

8. Encourage them to draw the pictures they saw or things they liked in the story (guide them to the Art Area)

9. Encourage them to repeat words, or point out words they do not know so you can help with meaning or understanding (have them repeat words or tell the story back to you, or make it up as they go)

9. Tell stories to each other orally (with or without books)

10. Include and provide various audio books and audio tools (these are equally as beneficial, and necessary for children with learning delays or differing abilities like dyslexia)

11. Use a felt board and felt stories to tell visual and oral stories

12. Use props (like puppets, figurines, or household items)

Materials for the Reading Area

These are suggestions for age appropriate material, but picture books and audio books are wonderful for any age. Most books will work as long as they are changed or rotated in an out regularly.

Toddlers
Ages 15 months-3

- Hidden picture, dress me, pop-up, board and cloth
- Simple, short story books (rich in pictures, hard cover books and board books are best for this age group)

Preschool - Kindergarten, Ages 3-4

- Animal stories
- Alphabet books
- Words and rhymes
- Stories about children's own life experiences
- Washing, dressing, bedtime routines, potty, grocery shopping

Ages 4-5

- Fairy tales
- Silly and wild stories
- Grocery shopping
- Body function stories
- Fire, ambulance, police, doctor, other
- Stories that deal with feelings
- Informational books (non-fiction)
- Mommy and Daddy, or family stories

Through Grade 1
Ages 5-7

- Real-event stories
- Insects: ants, butterflies, caterpillars, other
- Animals: dogs, cats, birds
- Poetry
- Emerging reader books

Writing Area

The Writing Area can be combined with the Art Area or its own space (depending on the age of your child, the space you have available, and what

interests your child). As discussed in the Art Area, when my children were very young, I used an easel for art activities.

The time spent painting was so short, and the art was primitive. I liked that they could stand and paint. Fine motor skills are not developed enough, and neither is their attention span great enough to sit and color for long periods of time, or work on small projects.

More advanced art begins once they reach kindergarten age and have mastered holding a crayon or pencil, and now have the attention span to color an detailed picture. When I found my oldest sitting for long periods writing, drawing pictures, and painting, I knew I needed to establish a quiet space out of the main playroom so she could sit and concentrate, focus, and explore. Once that happened, this space became the Writing Area.

To this day, I have it stocked with various colored pencils, markers, paints, crayons, and more. I also have a drawer full of more advanced drawing books, recycled paper, writing materials, old notebooks, construction paper, sticky notes, folders, and more.

Having a dedicated space to explore writing, crafting, and art encourages creativity and continues to develop fine motor mastery.

GETTING STARTED

1. **Table and Chairs**
2. **Paper supplies**
   (varied sizes and shapes of paper, coloring books)
3. **Writing and drawing tools**
   (crayons, markers, or colored pencils)

Materials for the Writing Area

- **Crayons**
- **Broad and fine-tip markers** (washable, non-toxic)
- **Pencils** (broad and narrow)
- **Rulers** (different sizes and shapes)
- **Envelopes** (various sizes, new or recycled)
- **Colored pencils**
- **Chalk**
- **Scissors**
- **Hole punchers**
- **Stapler**
- **Paper clips**
- **Clip board**
- **Erasers**

- **Tracing shapes** (mixed sizes)
- **Different types of tapes** (masking, painter's, scotch, colored, cellophane, other)
- **Grip guides** (pencil guides)
- **Post-it notes** (*children love these*)

- **Stickers**
- **Pencil sharpener**
- **Magnifying glasses**
- **Old keyboard, old computer, type-writer**
- **Other** (use your imagination)

White boards & white board erasable markers (no odor, nontoxic) are a wonderful alternative, large or small. Small white boards are often used in school for practicing and learning letters, writing, and more. White boards can be used with magnets or to write on (for easy clean up), when rotated in. I also had small white boards in the Writing Area to practice letters, or for easy clean up (these are great to take on car trips, too).

Brochures, magazines, marketing materials, and junk mail are all great to accumulate and use in the Art Area or Writing Area. These materials can be acquired while vacationing, at a tourist booth, libraries, from junk mail, or other free print circulations. Children love to look at pictures and cut things up (practicing their fine motor skills) and use these items for collages or pictures.

How to Set Up, Facilitate, & Use The Writing Area

The Writing Area is simple to facilitate once you have a space established and a stackable bin of supplies. Simply keep the area stocked with various materials. As discussed in the Art Area, let the children explore and create using the resources and tools available. **Refer to PART II: Art Area**, as many of these concepts and materials overlap and are combined.

Each day I would supply a type of base material such as paper, construction paper, cardboard, or other and supply tools such as scissors, hole punchers, coloring pages, glue, crayons, colored pencils, bingo daubers, or other.

Some days I would provide a structured or guided activity, like tracing letters or shapes, or making houses or dolls. Some days we did a special art craft for a holiday (for example, coloring Easter eggs). For Halloween, I would cut out pumpkin shapes or we would carve pumpkins. In the winter I would teach them how to make snowflakes or holiday cards. Some days I would take out glue and Popsicle sticks, or wooden bird houses, and paint to make a craft.

Once they are school age (fix and up), you can just provide access to all the resources. As mentioned before, even older children still need prompting, suggestions, or challenges. I still facilitate on days there is no school, by

taking out colored pencils and wrapping paper, or putting old magazines and scissors on top of the writing table with glue, for collages

Older children will require more advanced materials and activities and create much more elaborate crafts than younger children.

Listening Area

The Listening Area can be merged with and be part of the Reading Area, as a lot of space is not required. Everyone knows the importance of reading to a child daily, as discussed in the Reading Area, but this section

illustrates different ways of learning through audio. I highlight this as its own area to make sure it is understood as a fundamentally different space to facilitate.

Listening is an important part of development for auditorty processing, reading, cognition, comprehension, problem-solving, and speech and language. Children love to listen to music, people talking, or hearing stories! Music is also a form of art and a universal language.

Research has shown that there are areas in the brain that respond only to music, and these areas trigger our emotional responses and experience. Brain scans also show that different areas in the brain are activated when different types of music is played. Sounds like banging or crashing were shown to evoke unpleasant emotions, whereas melodies and harmonic sounds evoked pleasant feelings.

In this area there should be a child accessible CD player or digital audio player, a selection of music, and musical instruments. I first purchased a child-safe CD player so the children could explore and touch it. It is always

fun to push buttons. I would assist with the CDs to make sure they wouldn't get scratched but allowed the children to practice and play music when they wanted.

I also had small CD players with headphones

so one child could focus and listen to stories and books on tape without interruption or distraction. You can also label the players with stickers, red (OFF), and green (ON). Labels always enhance a learning experience.

Pure audio is one of the greatest ways to learn language, especially for

the evolving reader or children with speech delays or differing abilities.

My oldest child listened to the entire Magic Treehouse series for months before bed and read along when she was able. Even though my middle child was diagnosed with dyslexia, she consistently scored above average in language in early grades. I believe this is because of her early exposure to these resources. She has an advanced comprehension and vocabulary (despite her continued difficulties with the written word).

Having a variety of music and audio options also provides the greatest diversity and exposure during language development (to various voices, sounds, and even foreign languages).
I always had some type of music playing each day and a vast variety to choose from (songs in Spanish, Italian, Chinese, children's songs, top forty hits, opera, and more). I also played various books on tape and poetry readings. At first, I purchased CDs and books on tape, but again (as discussed in the Reading Area) realized this was a significant expense and found the library had many more option.

I also found one of the best opportunities I had for this was during car rides. I figured since we spent so much time in the car, I could do something positive with that time and keep their minds busy, even when their bodies had to be still. Learning can happen everywhere.

My children loved listening to stories as much as watching a movie, and I felt good I was encouraging something educational. They often listened quietly (and were learning), while I had the chance to make those necessary phone calls.

Various types of musical instruments are also important to have in this space. They can be left out or rotated in on the Center Activity Table. I started with a kit that had five items that children of any age could use, then added to this collection over time, and based on their interests. My oldest wanted a harp after a concert when she was four and a ukulele when she was older. My middle one loved flutes and bells. My youngest loved any type of drum he could bang.

GETTING STARTED

1. **Music player & headphones**
2. **Various audio books** (the library is the most affordable way to have a variety of listening resources)
3. **1 set of musical instruments or a Xylophone**
4. **2 scarves**

Materials for the Listening Area

- **Audio player**
- **Headphones** (noise canceling are great)
- **Various genres of music**
- **Audio books** (various types)
- **Drums** (various sizes and types)
- **Tambourine**
- **Xylophone**
- **Bells, bell bands, melody bells**
- **String instruments** (guitar, ukulele, other)

- **Kazoos**
- **Rhythm sticks**
- **Scarves**
- **Piano**
- **Maracas**
- **Flutes**
- **Streamers**
- **Wands**
- **Whistles**

- **Shakers and rattles** (you can even make these with rice kernels and toilet, recycled coffee tins, or paper towel tubes)
- **Other**

How to Set Up, Facilitate, & Use the Listening Area

1. Provide a variety of interesting and diverse music or sounds (daily, that are age appropriate)

2. Have different types of audio (genres of music, audio stories, poetry readings, singing, opera, talking, other)

3. Provide audio books to listen quietly on headphones while flipping pages (for younger children, make sure to get books that have a bell to indicate when to turn the page)

4. Bring books into the Reading Area (match the music, have themes, and use dress-up clothes in the House Area)

5. Explore different languages and cultures

6. Encourage your child to sing along (and sing along with them)

7. Select different music to dance to for movement time

8. Play musical instruments together (along with the harmony, tune, or make up your own sounds or songs)

9. Explore the sounds of different objects or instruments (bring in other items like pots and pans to experiment with)

Construction & Block Area

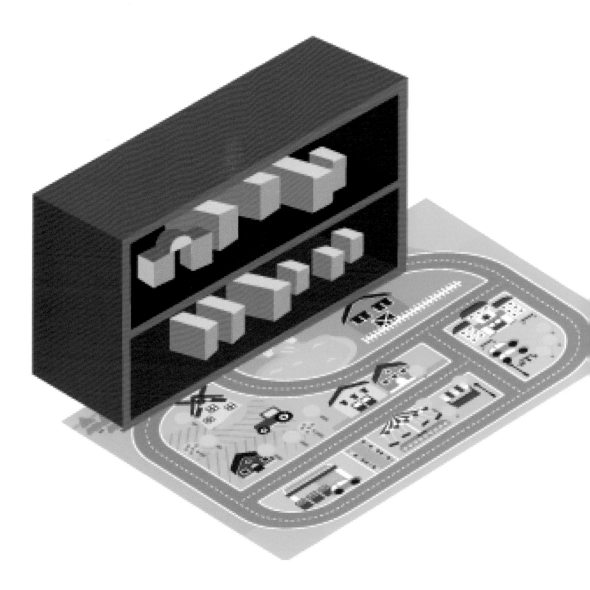

The Construction & Block Area is an area for building and construction (with objects and accessories for play). Working with various types of blocks stimulates the whole child.

A child uses their bodies, reasoning and logic, and problem solving in planning and building a structure. Working with blocks also promotes language development and creative thinking.

Playing with blocks and constructing requires hand-eye coordination, measurement, balance, and the ability to see and create patterns. Building can provoke memory like the shape of the church, spire, or the angled roof of a home. If there is more than one child playing it also calls for cooperation and respect. Many of the building resources overlap in this space with materials from the Center Activity Table.

Boys tend to prefer this learning area more than girls do, and in preschool settings, they spend most of their time in and out of this space. I had large cardboard blocks and extra-large plastic Legos for building, a bin of small blocks, and a construction table with construction equipment. I did not have a unit block collection that you will find in most preschools, until I acquired a set from a closing preschool. A new good set of blocks can be expensive. **Refer to Part III: Suggestions to Purchase Toys & Equipment.**

However, if you have more than one boy (or a girl more interested in cars, trucks, and building), I would make this a primary and separate space, and purchase a large block

set that comes with all the wooden block pieces in one purchase.

A flat surface or flat carpeting is best for blocks (exercise mats work great too). If you have space, provide two or three shelves to store the blocks and accessories.

Children will build towers and spaces to hide toys, especially cars. Children are very proud of their work and will want to show you what they build. Leave it set up for a while. All children love signs like "Do Not Touch" or "Keep Out". This makes it very clear to everyone at home, that the hard work is acknowledged It is important to have the children honor this with each other, especially if you have more than one child. After a day or so, have them dismantle it and put it away.

GETTING STARTED

1. Shelf for blocks

2. Set of unit blocks

3. Garage & 2 or 3 construction vehicles

4. 3 or 4 construction or service people (workers, other)

Materials for the Construction & Block Area

- **Set of unit blocks** (approximately $250 or check your on line marketplaces or yard sales)
- **Various types of garages**
- **Different types and sizes boats, planes, trains, tracks, ramps, other**
- **Figurines** (wooden, plastic, cloth, military, construction, service, super hero, other)
- **Construction vehicles & equipment or accessories**

(signs, cones, jersey barriers, other)
- **Road mats, maps or floor rugs**
- **Animals** (farm, sea, other)
- **Dominoes**
- **Jenga**
- **Lincoln Logs**
- **Erector Kits**
- **PVC piping and tubes** (toilet or paper towel tubes, for playing with cars and balls)
- **Various sizes and types of building manipulatives and blocks** (hollow blocks, 100-piece wooden blocks, cardboard blocks, ABC blocks, 3D blocks, interlocking, motorized, other)
- **Magnet Tiles, Magnet Buildings Blocks, Magnet Sticks, Magnet Balls**
- **Other**

How to Set Up, Facilitate, & Use Construction & Block Area

1. Alternate a variety of construction options and figurines (rotate in manipulatives from the Center Activity Table learning area, such as stacking cups or magnetic tiles and balls)

2. Have different types of block sizes and building options

3. Talk about the objects and architecture; names, colors, patterns, shapes, numbers, sizes ("This is a triangle" or "This is a roof")

4. Show different options for construction (stacking or aligning shapes a different way)

5. Help your children build (build a tower or start a tower, then ask them to complete the tower)

6. Set up the figures in a construction site in the right places (police officer directing traffic, cement truck in the center of the building area)

7. Suggest what items are used for, show how it moves, and what it does (the cement truck pours concrete for the basement for the foundation of a building)

8. Play with them, be a character (be a police officer figurine during a rescue)

9. Help when a child is having trouble, after trying many

times (show them how to operate a crane correctly)

10. Commend a pattern or successful completion of a task ("What a great tower you made!") **and leave it set up to be admired**

11. Be curious about their discoveries (ask what they figured out or learned, remembered, or what things are; square, triangle, crane)

Dollhouse Area

This is not a typical learning area that is separated from the House Area in a preschool center, but I separate it here because a large dollhouse

is a great space to play for children, even boys (especially if space is limited and you cannot fit a kitchen or some of the other materials mentioned). A large dollhouse is a tiny world of imagination.

A dollhouse targets many of the same areas of learning that are targeted in the House Area. Children will experience the same concepts, on a different level and in a different way. **Refer to Part II: House Area**.

Besides the normal things that one can imagine with a dollhouse, having it as its own space in the playroom establishes it as a separate place to play. If you have more than one child, as well as children with varying interests, this allows them to play separately even if they are in the same room.

All the playhouses and dollhouses I acquired (mostly outfitted), I bought at yard sales or picked up on the side of the road. Bleach and soap works wonders! Most are super expensive to buy new with all the pieces and I wanted to be able to rotate different ones in the space to add variety. I had at least ten different sizes and options. The scenarios they allow children to create are what matters.

As my two girls reached school age, this was one of the most frequently played with areas in the playroom. I also put one in each of their rooms that were added over the years. My oldest played Flexi-Barbies with her house, and my youngest played with her Shopkins and small dolls.

Over time, we accumulated a lot of furniture, pieces and sets, as well as miscellaneous items and clothes.

GETTING STARTED

1. **A dollhouse**
2. **A set of small dolls**
   (family or variety)
3. **5 to 10 pieces of furniture**

Materials for the Dollhouse Area

- **Various houses**
- **Different types of figurines & dolls**
- **Dress up clothing**
- **Chairs**
- **Tables**
- **Beds, cribs, desks**
- **Sinks, toilets**
- **Plants**
- **Lamps**
- **Pictures**
- **TV's**
- **Refrigerator**

- **Blankets, towels, rugs**
- **Phones, radios**
- **Computers**
- **Stove**
- **Microwave**
- **Pots, pans**
- **Vacuum, mop**
- **Blender**
- **Camping supplies**
- **Food items**
- **Bath items** (shower, tub, toiler, sink, other)
- **Vehicles** (cars, trucks, camper, other)
- **Other**

How to Set Up, Facilitate, & Use the Dollhouse Area

There is not much facilitation required, other than set up. My girls loved when they would come down to their play area (at any age), and I would have the whole dollhouse staged for play. Siblings will often play here quietly together and role play, but they will also often play separately, and alone.

1. Supply different options of houses and figurines

2. Talk about the objects (chair, table, bed)

3. Set up the figures in the houses, in the right places (the parent at the kitchen stove, the children in their beds)

4. Play with them, be a character (the grandfather, child, cat)

5. Help with an activity

6. Provide or make homemade houses or items (cut blankets, rugs, or curtains out of old fabric, make your own dollhouses out of cardboard boxes and recyclables using bottle caps for tables, and so on)

7. Refer to Part II: House Area for additional suggestions and ideas

Sensory Table

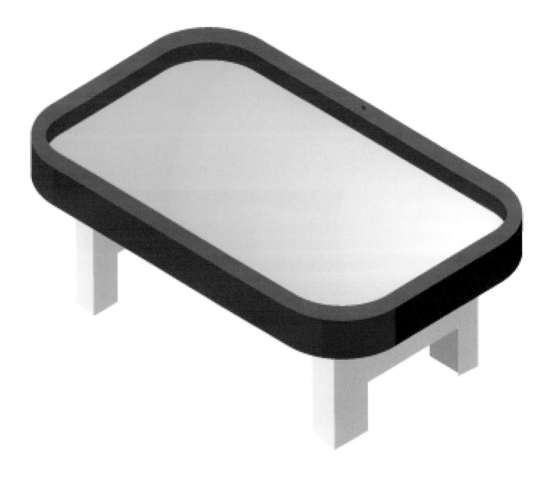

Sensory tables are for exploration and discovery, and experimentation with elements such as earth and water. Children investigate, explore, create, and play. So much learning takes place from sensory exploration like developing math and science concepts, fine motor skills, and more.

Children learn how water and elements move, and aspects of things like gravity with hands-on experience, by pouring and feeling it.

Children learn through touch how to manipulate objects within their environments. A sensory table may seem like a simple resource but when it is used properly, it is one of the most powerful learning tools an early educator or parent can provide.

I purchased two different sized Sensory Tables from discountschoolsupply.com; one small blue one (eighteen inches high) for $105 when the children were very small and another larger red one (twenty-four inches high with an eight-inch deep tub) for $150 when my oldest turned four. The size does matter, as toddlers will not be able to reach a larger table. The child

should be able to stand up naturally, with their arms able to easily reach over, so their hands can touch the surface.

A sensory table does not require elaborate planning or fancy projects to keep children interested. I have seen some neat ideas and books on fancy activities for sensory play, but with three children I rarely had the time to set up and do them. Instead, I used simple things like water or sand as a base and added other items they could use their imaginations with.

I did not have a dedicated space for the table. It moved regularly and was used inside or outside, depending on the activity, season, or weather. Sometimes I left it outside for weeks in the driveway, when the weather was warm, for outdoor play. I alternated with beach sand that I carried home in a bucket from the ocean. *Beach sand is very fine and great for straining and pouring (and free).*

Water play is simple, easy, and effective (especially during hot sum-

mer weeks). Set it up in the driveway or yard and fill it with kitchen measuring cups, dish soap, a few plastic storage containers, plastic syringes from CVS, and a hose. It will host hours of entertainment and fun with water games, car washes, pouring jobs, splashing, water fights, bathing, and more.

Combine a hose or a sprinkler, an outdoor plastic kitchen, a sensory table and a few buckets and it will transform any driveway into a water park. Often my children would put the water table on the ground, fill it, sit or lie in it, dump it to make a stream, pretend it was a pool or boat, or other. Most of these scenarios my children came up with on their own, I just provided the tools.

We also mixed up the activities with bubbles, food coloring, sponges, Q-tips, old rags, sprayers, even paint brushes. Cutting up sponges or rags into small pieces adds a fun element of play, whether playing car wash with matchbox cars, their bicycles, or helping you wash your car.

Children love things their size,

like little bars of soap. Children can practice giving their dolls or toys a bath (or "pretend" if a doll is not allowed to get wet).

Regardless of the material, whether it is sand, water, snow, or pasta, all you have to do to change it regularly and throw in different work tools; empty bottles, bowls, recyclables, sifters, measuring cups and spoon, medicine dispensers, and more.

Children love anything that can measure, fill, dump, splash, shoot water (like a water gun, turkey baster, or medicine dispenser), sift, poke, pour, squirt, squeeze, or simply hold whatever substance there is.

Sometimes I would hide things in the sand or snow to find, and create an adventure (coins or smooth glass pieces from a mosaic kit I never used). The girls pretended they were pirates finding treasure. They loved doing this, using the strainers or just digging in the sand with their fingers. Then they would take turns hiding the "jewels" and finding them. These jewels also got sorted, organized, and placed in a hierarchy of most valuable to least valuable (all without my intervention).

I rotated in marbles and plastic dinosaurs and dinosaur bones (from another kit we never used). This turned into pretending they were archaeologists. I was in shock when my oldest used that word at the age of six.

I found a great idea at a fair I attended, where a huge sandbox was filled with dried out corn! Dried corn was a completely different element to pour, drive trucks on, and just feel. My kids loved it. You can buy corn or even birdseed at any local farm or animal supply

store. Be sure to use it outside first because these are super dusty.

I often incorporated other props when using the Sensory Table, to change the scenarios, like incorporating a small baby pool and different-sized buckets or bins. I always had old plastic kitchens that I kept outside (again, that I found on the side of the road).

Often when the Sensory Table was full of sand, a few buckets and a hose,

the kitchen would change from pretend play to experimental play of cooking with dirt, rocks, and sticks! Mud pies, nature soups, dirt sandwiches, all mixed with grass, rocks, and twigs will create an absolute mess, but little scientific minds will be growing and flourishing.

During indoor play and colder days, I would set up the sensory table in the kitchen or mudroom. I tried to use the Sensory Table at least twice a week. I filled the table with water, sand, playdough, Floam, magic sand, snow, leaves, pasta, rocks, shaving cream, bubbles, flour, corn, rice, or other materials (anything that is safe to touch and explore with little fingers). Even collecting acorns in the Fall works, they are plentiful.

Children love to drink the water, eat the snow or pasta, even raw. Make sure the items are clean and edible, if edible. If they are not, make sure that the child is old enough to know not to put the items in their mouth.

Water is the easiest to set up and the most readily available resource. Children never seem to get bored playing with water, even older children. Adding food coloring or bubbles is a simple way to change the experience.

In the winter snow can be another easy and readily available source. Playing and eating cold snow is a wonderful sensory activity. Food coloring is also great in snow. Maple syrup is fun and tasyt to add to snow. Heating the syrup makes the snow melt just a little and makes a great sticky treat (not too hot or it will melt the snow and can burn)! Scoop up with little spoons or Popsicle sticks.

Adults do not need to teach or orchestrate play with sensory tables, just facilitate with the right tools (and make sure for small children the materials are safe and age-appropriate) and let children explore and discover!

Get creative and just throw things in and watch the children explore! Adding accessories used in the Sensory Table can also transform bath time into hours of fun and learning over standard tub toys. Children love to manipulate, experiment, discover, measure, and pour with little hands and fingers!

GETTING STARTED

1. **Sensory table or large bin**
2. **1 base material** (water, sand, or other)
3. **1 set of measuring cups and spoons**

Materials for the Sensory Table

- **Water**
- **Snow**
- **Birdseed**
- **Rice**
- **Corn**
- **Pasta**
- **Flour**
- **Sand**
- **Rocks**

- **Things that fill, dump, splash, or shoot water** (funnels, tubing, spray bottles, syringes, sponges, rags, turkey baster, medicine dispensers from CVS, or other)

- **Measuring cups**
- **Measuring spoons**
- **Kitchen utensils**
- **Tweezers and egg cartons for sorting**
- **Funnels, tubing, basters**
- **Marbles, coins**
- **Mosaic glass, seashells**
- **Other small items** (to hide and find)
- **Sifters, strainers, colanders**
- **Playdough tools**
- **Other**

How to Set Up, Facilitate, & Use the Sensory Table

A sensory table does not need much facilitation once the materials have been set up! Simply provide the resources and watch hours of learning and exploration begin!

1. Set up a base material and tools

2. Provide various tools for exploration and discovery

3. Discuss science concepts (warm water versus cold water, ice crystals, rock layers, other)

4. Discuss what earth elements are and where they come from (snow is frozen water crystals)

5. Facilitate imagination games (miners, archaeologists, treasure hunters to find the rare blue gem, other)

Outdoor Area

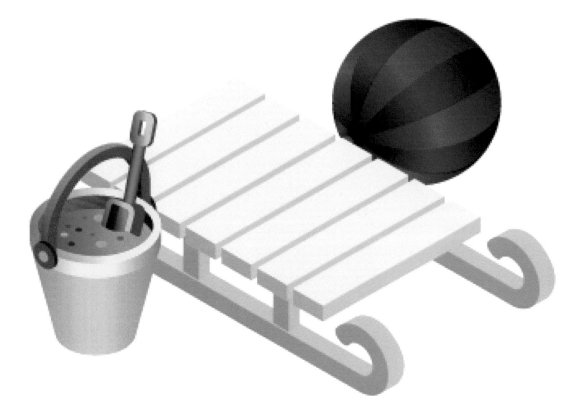

Having a safe outdoor play area for children is extremely important. Children should play outside for at least one hour every day or more!

Recent studies have found that children who played in dirt had stronger immune systems and were less likely to be obese than those who didn't. It helps their immune system become more robust and boosts their mood. Children who can run and play outside not only burn off a lot of energy, but develop healthy appetites and sleep better.

An outdoor play structure or swing set with a slide is wonderful for young children, but if you do not have the space, just setting up or assigning an outdoor play area is enough. My children had a swing set in the back yard. When they were small, I encouraged them to climb up and slide down the slide or pump the swings. But the older they became, the less interested, and it simply became a fort for hiding.

When we needed a change of scenery, we often went to one of the many playgrounds nearby (the elementary school or local park). If you have limited outdoor play space, taking children to public places is just as beneficial and a great addition to a daily routine.

I did purchase a wonderful climbing structure that I highly recommend. It turned out to be a great investment, and much cheaper than a swing set

(that can cost thousands of dollars). It is a five-foot Lifetime Geometric Dome Climber Play Center. It retails for $249 (two adults are needed to assemble). It is a dome that children can climb or hang from. It is super sturdy. It is also a year-round piece of equipment. The children use it constantly in many ways and play scenarios. In the winter we use it as an igloo by covering it with a tarp. I set it up on the other side of the house, away from the swing set, to establish its own play space.

As with the learning areas inside the house, setting up different areas outside encourages and creates different spaces to play. This entices children to

naturally move around, and it feels new when it hasn't been used for a while.

I established a resource area in the garage. I have a bin of materials and toys that the children can use at their discretion (outdoor paints, bubbles, various ball, bats, jump ropes, buckets, beach toys, and more). This is another space that we still use!

As discussed in the Sensory Table and Art Area section, I also incorporated toys from these areas that could get wet. Outdoor paints and painting with water is also fun. Bubbles are always a huge hit!

The children all had tricycles when they were small and bicycles and scooters as they got older (and proper safety gear). Now, we take our bikes to the school to ride since our roads are not safe.

When my children were young, I drew various tracks and obstacle courses on my driveway with chalk. I drew roads and challenges, often us-

ing cones or objects to navigate or avoid. I set up big circles (and made the paths more difficult as they got older and mastered riding). I created pretend cities with places to stop at, as they rode around (Starbucks, grocery store, bank, school, other). I created challenges using

pretend signs and symbols to teach concepts like "Stop" and "Go". I used chalk to draw and create games like hopscotch, hop through a maze, throw the rock and hit the line, four-square, and more.

Chalk is a must have in any outdoor play space! It is inexpensive and provides limitless opportunities! Children will draw constantly if there is a bucket of chalk available and a hard surface (I also kept chalk in my basement area).

Having outdoor resources in a bin and facilitating these types of activities keeps children interested and busy outside (even if you do not have a large outdoor area). Winters can be long in New England but I bundled mine up and sent them outside every day, even if only lasted twenty minutes. Often getting on all the winter gear takes just as long.

GETTING STARTED

1. **Define an outdoor area**
2. **Set up a large plastic bin or tub**
3. **Three balls** (different sizes)
4. **One jump rope**
5. **One bundle of chalk**

Materials for the Outdoor Area

- **Climbing structure**
- **Swing set**
- **Sandbox**
- **Small baby pool**
- **Sensory table**
- **Beach toys**
- **Bats & gloves**
- **Gloves**
- **Buckets** (various sizes)
- **Old paint brushes**
- **Bicycles and helmet**
- **Scooters**
- **Hose** (for warmer months)
- **Different-size and types of balls** (basketballs, kickball, tennis balls, blow-up balls, plastic balls, other)
- **Roller blades**
- **Sleds**
- **Chalk**
- **Bubbles**
- **Bubble wands & trays**
- **Hula hoops**
- **Water guns**
- **Sprayers**
- **Jump ropes**
- **Hop Balls**
- **Other**

How to Set Up, Facilitate, & Use the Outdoor Area

Facilitating outdoor play is just as important as indoor play, and setting up outdoor areas and different play spaces keeps them active and having fun!

1. Identify an area or designated areas for outdoor play (for example, use chalk to highlight the area, or cones if small children are riding bikes to provide a buffer)

2. Go outside for an hour every day (play, walk, hike)

3. Facilitate games and activities

4. Review outside play area rules (safety, boundaries, other)

5. Set up a storage bin of various materials and toy options that are easily accessible (bats, balls, frisbees, jump ropes, other)

6. Provide equipment such as swing sets or climbing structures (or access to them)

7. Provide safety equipment (helmets, padding, cones, barriers, other)

8. Encourage children to move their bodies and explore nature (lift up rocks, find bugs, identify types of leaves)

9. Teach about the weather and environment (examine different parts of the environment; birds, insects, trees)

PART III

QUICK GUIDE: Rotation of Toys & Learning Areas

DAILY ROTATION

1. **One art activity** - *Art Area*
2. **One collection of figures** - *Center Activity Table or Construction & Block Area*
3. **One playhouse** *Center Activity Table or Construction & Block Area*
4. **Two to three manipulatives** - *Center Activity Table or Construction & Block Area*
5. **Various books** - *Reading Area*
6. **A varitery of music or sounds** - *Listening Area*
7. **Two to five puzzles** - *Center Activity Table, Writing Area, or your kitchen table*
8. **Playdough or sand & sets of playdough tools** - *Center Activity Table, Sensory Table, or your kitchen table*

BI-WEEKLY OR WEEKLY *(or other, depending on interest and use)*

1. **One to two board games** - *Center Activity Table, Writing Area, or your kitchen table*
2. **One to two matching game** - *Center Activity Table, Writing Area, or your kitchen table*
3. **Medical supplies** - *Center Activity Table or House Area*
4. **One to two sports equipment** - *Climbing and Movement Area*
5. **One playhouse or tent** - *Playhouse Area*

How to Structure a Day Suggestions

The daily suggested schedule is broken into time blocks, beginning around eight a.m. and ending at around five p.m. Young children are not always aware of time but do follow natural rhythms throughout the day from waking with the sun to needing time to rest. Children with a routine will begin to recognize and expect that each day. **Refer to PART I-II: Preparedness and PART I-II: Transition Time**.

For instance, they know they will go outside after lunch and begin to look forward to that time, as well as a story before bed. If I do not read my children a story before bed (even an extremely short story), it takes them twice as long to fall asleep. My almost eleven and ten-year-old still ask me to read to them before bed. I try to skip schoolwork and read books they enjoy, to continue to foster their love of stories. This is simply the trigger in their brain they are accustomed to, that it is time to fall asleep.

This time allotment is meant to be a guide. Younger children have shorter attention spans than older children but giving at least one to two hours in the morning for free play to explore is a great window.

The schedule and structure can be adjusted to suit your needs, and those of your children. This schedule aims to target the learning domains and necessary areas of development, as well as establish a routine in alignment with the natural rhythms of a child.

A TYPICAL DAY

1. **Free play** (2 hours)
2. **Art activity** (30 minutes to 1 hour)
3. **Reading or listening** (30 minutes to 1 hour)
4. **Movement: Indoor play** (30 minutes) **or Outdoor play** (1 to 2 hours), this will vary and increases with age
5. **Lunch/Show** (30 minutes)
6. **Reading** (10 to 30 minutes)
7. **Rest** (20 to 30 minutes)/**Nap** (one to two hours)
8. **Structured activity** (30 minutes to 1 hour)
9. **Free play** (1 to 2 hours)

The day should begin with free play, allowing the child or children to simply explore the room you have set up and play freely without intervention, unless needed. This is when a child wakes up and enters the room.

When they are small, all the objects are important jobs to do and should await them.

The child will usually start to play with the Center Activity Table toys that have been set out, and then wander around to the other learning areas, especially if there are fresh toys awaiting.

This is a wonderful time for you to make breakfast, vacuum, or do laundry! I would also leave an art project set up.

The CD was always playing music or songs but during the dedicated time for Reading and Listening, I would either read a story or put an audio book. I usually left three or four books out on the floor, even though I rotated the books in the bookcase, to encourage use.

Lunchtime was the one time I had the television on. Until around six-years-old, my children did not have screen time other than a show before lunch and dinner. My children were very active, and this was a form of rest before lunch. I absolutely loved Curious George. It is a phenomenal show that exposes young children to science and math concepts in a fun and playful manner. I would let my children watch an episode while I was making lunch, and often during lunch. Some will argue children should not eat in front of a TV, but it worked for mine (Curious George, Sesame Street, Caillou, The Berenstain Bears, Blues Clues, other).

Rest time is a very important time of the day for a child. Even older children who no longer nap need quiet time to process information from

the day and rest their growing bodies. A child's mind works two to three times as hard as ours do!

Homemade Playdough Recipe

INGREDIENTS:

- Food coloring, optional
- 2 cups all-purpose flour
- 3/4 cup salt
- 4 teaspoons cream of tartar
- 2 cups lukewarm water
- 2 Tablespoons of vegetable oil (coconut oil works too)

1. In a large bowl, combine all of your dry ingredients (flour, salt, cream of tartar), **and mix well.**

2. Combine food coloring with the water in a cooking pot, then add the vegetable oil.

3. Mix the dry ingredients into the pot until mixed well.

4. Cook over medium to low heat, until the dough starts to take form, and becomes dry.

5. When it starts to form a ball, remove it from the stove. Let the dough cool first before touching.

6. Once cooled, knead the dough for 5 minutes to make it soft. Continue kneading for another 5 minutes, until soft. If it is too dry add a little more oil and knead it in.

Suggestions to Purchase Toys & Equipment

- **Constructive Playthings, Educational Supplies and Learning** www.constructiveplaythings.com
- **Discount School Supply** www.discountschoolsupply.com
- **Early Childhood Manufacturers Direct** www.schoolspecialty.com/early-childhood
- **Kaplan, Teaching Supplies and Childcare Resources** www.kaplanco.com
- **Learning Toys Lakeshore** www.lakeshorelearning.com
- **Play** www.play.com
- **Toys That Are Good for Your Children and for the Environment** www.imaginetoys.com/arts-crafts-toys
- **Safari** www.safariltd.com
- **School Outfitters** www.schooloutfitters.com

Resources

- **Author Jodi Dee, Parenting** www.jodidee.com/blogs/parenting
- **Center on Developing Child** www.developingchild.harvard.edu
- **The Creative Curriculum for Preschool**
  www.teachingstrategies.com
- **Early Childhood News** www.earlychildhoodnews.com
- **Early Learning Services** www.rcoe.us/early-learning-services
- **Exchange - The Early Childhood Leaders Magazine**
  www.childcareexchange.com
- **Kaplan, Teaching Supplies and Childcare Resources**
  www.kaplanco.com
- **National Association for the Education of Young Children**
  www.naeyc.org & **TYC - Teaching Young Children Magazine**
- **National Association for Early Learning Leaders**
  www.earlylearningleaders.org
- **National Association for Family Childcare** www.nafcc.org
- **Massachusetts Department of Early Education & Care**
  www.mass.gov/orgs/department-of-early-education
- **Red Leaf Press** www.redleafpress.org
- **Scholastic Learn at Home**
  www.scholastic.com/parents/school-success/home-learning-
  resources.html
- **Teachers College Press** www.tcpress.com
- **US Department of Education** www.ed.gov
- **Zero to Three** www.zerotothree.org

Glossary

Accredited Early Learning Programs: An accredited program is a qualified early education and childcare service. These include center-based and family childcare programs: National Association for the Education of Young Children, for center-based and National Association for Family Care, for home-based programs.

ADD: Attention Deficit Disorder: A disorder that challenges a child's ability to focus on task for extended periods of time.

ADHD: Attention Deficit Hyperactivity Disorder: A disorder that challenges a child's ability to focus (as in ADD), but also involves restlessness and increased or constant body movement (such as fidgeting).

Associate Play: A stage of development where a child begins to play next to other children and observe, but not engage in play with them..

Building Blocks of Math: Children need to grasp math concepts before performing math operations. For example, games such as rolling the dice, counting dots, and learning 'more or less' precedes addition and subtraction. Building with blocks and Legos also establishes geometry concepts.

Busy Bees Preschool Center: The place where Jodi Dee grew up and learned how to design the environment for Create a Home of Learning.

Centers: Dedicated areas in an accredited preschool that target the learning domains of a developing child.

Cognitive: The reasoning brain function where for example, we might ask "What if ..." and other open-ended questions.

Construction of Knowledge: Children build an understanding of the world around them by exposure to their immediate physical, language and social/emotional environment.

Cooperative Play: The stage in development when child begin to engage and play together with other children towards a common goal.

Curriculum Frameworks & National Standards for Early Learning: Refers to national curriculum components and learning standards for early and elementary age students.

Developmental Ranges: Each child has a unique trajectory for growth and development. One child may walk at 12 months while another walks at 10 months of age. One child may read at age 5 while another may read at age 7.

Emotional Connection: A child's attachment to the people in his/her life.

Expressive Language: The spoken word.

Eye-hand coordination: A child's ability to perform a task such as cutting with scissors, using eyes to see, and hands to cut.

Facilitator: The person who creates or sets up a learning environment.

Fine Motor or Small Muscle: The muscles in our fingers and hands.

Free Play or Unstructured Play: A child's individual choice of activity (puzzles, dolls, painting, etc.), which is not directed by an adult facilitator.

Gross or Large Muscle: Movement of the muscles in the arms, legs, and/or whole-body movement.

Integrated Learning: Activities that are designed to address more than one area of developmental domain at a time.

Learning Connections: A child's understanding of concepts. For example, with the concept of measurement, a cat is smaller than a horse, a rock is heavier than a feather and so on.

Learning Domains: This refers to the following areas of development: physical, social, emotional, cognitive and language and literacy.

Manipulatives: A term early educators use for a collection of activities and toys that are manipulated; Legos, blocks, connectors, etc.

National Association for the Education of Young Children: A national association for quality early education and care services, for center-based childcare services.

National Association of Family Childcare Programs: A national association for quality early education and care services, for family-based childcare services.

Open-Ended Toys: Materials that are process-oriented, not product-oriented. Building with Legos is an open-ended activity while making a puzzle can only be made one way.

Open-Ended Questions: Question preceded with the words who, what, where, when and how. "What color is this?" is not an open-ended question whereas, "What did you eat for breakfast today?"

Parallel Play: When two children are playing side by side, without any interaction or intention of interaction.

Phonetic: The reference of learning how to read and spell by the sound of the spoken word. For example, "Kandy kanes hang on the fireplase man til".

Practice Coordination: The repetitive exercise of using our large or small muscles, for example, doing jumping jacks or cutting with scissors

Receptive Language: The spoken word we hear.

Secure Base: A place where a child feels safe.

Sequencing Skills: Placing things in order of occurrence, such as we turn on the tap for water, we fill the glass with water, and then we drink the water from the glass.

Solitary Play/Independent Play: Play by oneself without interaction with others.

Spatial Reasoning: Knowing where you are or where you put things, in space and in relation to something else, or the ability to understand and remember the relationship of one object to another.

Structured Play: Play with rules. It could be game of catch or a board game.

Transition Time: A period of time when moving from one activity to another. Examples include handwashing to breakfast or breakfast to free play, or indoors to outdoors.

Unstructured Play: Unstructured play is when a child is provided (usually open ended) toys or materials, to use or do whatever they choose with them (in a safe way).

References

Ambron, S., Salkind, N. (1987). Child Development, 5th ed. New York: CBS College Publishing

Beneke, S., Helm, J. (2003). The Power of Projects. New York: Teachers College Press

Berke, Laura E., Winsler, A. (1995) Scaffolding Children's Learning: Vygotsky and Early Childhood Education. Washington, DC: National Association for the Education of Young Children

Bronson, M. (1995). The Right Stuff for Children Birth to 8. Washington, DC: National Association for the Education of Young Children

Chrisman, K., Couchenour, D. (2002). Healthy Sexuality Development. Washington, DC: National Association for the Education of Young Children

Colker, L., Dodge, D., Heroman, C. (2002). The Creative Curriculum for Preschool, 4th ed. Washington, DC: Teaching Strategies

Colker, L., Dodge, D., Heroman, C. (2002). The Creative Curriculum: Connecting Content, Teaching, and Learning. Washington, DC: Teaching Strategies

Massachusetts Department of Education (2003). Guidelines for Preschool Learning Experiences. Boston, MA. Office of School of Readiness (this version has been updated)

Engel, B., Gronlund, G., (2001) Focused Portfolios. St. Paul, MN: RedLeaf Press

Heidemann, S., Hewitt, D. (1992). Pathways to Play: Developing Play Skills in Young Children. St. Paul, MN: RedLeaf Press

Hirsch, E. S. (Ed). (1996). The Block Book. Washington, DC: National

Association for the Education of Young Children

Klugman, E., Smilansky, S. (Ed.). (1990). Children's Play and Learning. New York: Teachers College

Jones, E., Nimmo, J. (1994) Emergent Curriculum. Washington, DC: National Association for the Education of Young Children

National Association for the Education of Young Children (2019). Early Learning Standards, Creating the Conditions for Success. Washington, DC: National Association for the Education of Young Children

Acknowledgements

I want to thank my mother, Cecile Tousignant for all her knowledge, experience, and support, not only for sharing her life's work with me, but for helping to share it with all of you. Through years of recommendations, ideas

for my own children, millions of questions, and finally edits of this material, it is finished.

I thank my father, David Tousignant, who supported my mother in building her top-notch center and in helping run her preschool for all the years he did, as part of our home.

I thank my children, Aria, Aiza, and Austin, who taught me infinite love. I could not be more proud of the people they have become and are becoming. It has been such a gift to be able to facilitate their growth and learning, and to watch them evolve into capable and competent young beings. It certainly was not always easy, but I wouldn't change any of it. I love you with all my heart.

I thank my ex-husband, Chad Healy, for supporting this process despite our separation, and continuing to use many of these resources and techniques in his home.

And finally, my oldest daugther Aria and her friend Zoey Szydlik for last minute editing (two very talented young women)!

About the Author

Author Jodi Dee is a multi-award winning Author, regular columnist for Bay State Parent Magazine, and an avid blogger. She is a mother of three with more than 20 years' experience in early childhood and education.

Jodi has a Bachelor of Arts in Psychology & History and a Master's in Education from Clark University. She is a passionate advocate and teacher of self-love, emotional maturity, early childhood education, and empowering children to learn through creativity, independence, and self-exploration and discovery.

Jodi's children's books The Dirt Girl, The Little Green Jacket, and her Jesse True series have won multiple awards in multiple categories; including the Purple Dragonfly Book Awards, National Indie Books Awards, International Book Awards, American Fiction Awards, Next Generation Indie Books Awards, and more.

Visit Jodi Dee for additional rich content, free downloads, articles, and more at her website jodidee.com or follow her on social media platforms @jodidee or @authorjodidee.

More Books by Author Jodi Dee

When Zafera goes to school for the first time, all the children laugh and tease. But Zafera does not understand, so she just smiles. A beautiful story about shining bright because our differences are our greatest gifts. And if you do, others will eventually see your light. *"A must have for all children!"*, *"Spectacular!"*, *"Wow!"*, *"Timeless."*

The Little Green jacket is a story based on true events about a little green jacket that travels through the lives of different children, who live in very different places, and ends up on the other side of the world after a natural disaster. Find out how the little green jacket experiences being a donation and the importance, power, and magic of giving! A true all-American classic that showcases the culture of donations and how it can change lives. *"An amazing piece of literature!"*, *"So impressed, it's universal!"*, *"Destined to become a classic!"*

Jesse True is just a normal little boy, until one day he starts changing color based on how he feels. Now, Jesse cannot hide his feelings or his truth. Join Jesse in his adventures as he experiences normal everyday things children do, trying to navigate his feelings with his new found super power! There are four books in the series with more to come! *"All children should have this resource!"*, *"Powerful!"*